HOW I GOT THIS WAY
AND WHAT TO DO ABOUT IT

by

Sterling Grant Ellsworth, Ph.D.

Contents

Preface   v

One   *Seeds of Self*   1

Part One   **Know Your Enemy**
Two   *The Substitute Self*   7
Three   *Some Styles of the False Self*   19
Four   *Bodies or Beings*   38

Part Two   **Conquer Your Enemy**
Five   *Real Love Supplies*   53
Six   *Real Love Versus Cheap Substitutes*   81
Seven   *Love Supplies From Within*   93
Eight   *Real Love Supplies and Romance*   119

Part Three   **Conclusion**
Nine   *The Real You*   127
Ten   *Sterling Quotes*   131

Preface

Twenty-five years ago I realized my patients needed a short, easy-to-read summary of the concepts that would help them heal themselves. Some of my patients even provided typed scripts of my talks that they had taped. The earliest one was a little booklet called "Precious Self."

Then Susan Roylance, from Washington, helped combine all of those talks into *A Tale Of Two Selves*. This little book greatly aided and sped up many people's counseling here and else where.

Later on, in the late 1970s, we enlarged our little book and called it *To Know Me Is To Love Me*, taken from the great saying by Snoopy. Carol Emily Ellsworth was the real writer/ editor of that version. She extracted the information from my tapes, albums and other sources to write the book.

Now, I have decided to revise it myself with the help of Keith and Ann Terry. I appreciate their help so much and also my wife Anne, who has encouraged me in this so very much.

This present work is not exhaustive or academic, but rather it is for the ordinary person who wants to be better than he is already.

The new book is full of metaphors and one liners. Its purpose is to clarify and motivate. It is intended to be a short and sweet book, designed to help the common person who usually seeks counseling on an out patient basis.

It is an introductory book only, especially for those who want to go further in reading specialty books on self help. Many works abound. These books are more exhaustive, academic, and scientific than mine. They are available to the public and certainly worth reading. But most people are not that interested.

In this book I try to show how to find your real self, both present and past. This will help us to run our bodies in the present and future. The whole aim is to help us be the person we really are, not the false survival self of the past.

The false self that I write about is the cause of most of the complaints people have who come to me for counseling.

No one has come from a perfect family where *all* our real feelings were honored and revered. Each of us, in order to learn and grow, has had to live partly or mostly in a false self, while our real self took a back seat. In order to survive we had to feel someone else's feelings and not our own so much. Our human feeling identity seed had to be partly abandoned. False identity styles like pleaser, caretaker, rebel, perfectionist, workaholic, and depressed emerged, leaving us afraid, hurt, sad, and angry.

When love supplies come into your life from a therapist, or others who want to help, you learn to get love from your real self and God. You then can forsake your false survival self and be who you really are. This can happen to you. It has already happened to thousands of people to some degree. Why couldn't one of them be you?

I think it can happen to any person who wants to do this badly enough. You will have to work and play at it, however the results will be great happiness and joy. You'll be in love with your life, even in adversity and have greater understanding of all things. This approach to life gives us great enrichment and passionate excitement in our marriages. Also, it gives us great joy in our relationships with our children and friends. It will certainly boost your career outside the home.

I hope this little book helps you in your journey.

Dr. Sterling Ellsworth — 1995

Chapter One
Seeds of Self

Have you ever noticed how many seeds are in an apple? It is not really hard to count them—most apples have about five seeds. But who could count the number of potential apples in a single seed? It is impossible! Its potential is for millions of apples. They exist in each little seed; with the proper opportunity to develop, each can actualize this identity potential.

But if you eat the apple and throw the core out the window onto the freeway, splat! That is the end! All that great potential lies smashed on the freeway. Tossing the seeds stifles growth and potential for millions of apples. Those marvelous, little seeds require the kind of nurturing that matches their identity. Given such disregard, those wonderful, delicious apples will never grow.

Seeds Inside Self

Inside each of us is our *human identity seed*. Like an apple seed, each little baby possesses a fantastic potential in a tiny, ready-to-develop state. A beautiful heavenly being enlivens the physical body of every newborn baby and gives identity to the physical body. The spirit self is the "me" we talk about when we identify our feelings, thoughts, or desires; it is the alive, feeling, and thinking part of us that dwells inside our bodies. It is out of sight, yet very much there inside our being. What a precious, wonderful self we have inside. Nothing in all the world can compare to that inner self.

Some call it the inside self, the soul, the real self, or true self, even the primary self.

On the other end of life, we know from recent studies on death and dying that many people have been declared clinically dead, but have been revived after a few minutes. And their experiences during that short time out of the body have convinced them that the true human identity—the *real self*—is actually not the same thing as the body.

In fact, once their inner self or spirits leave their bodies, they speak of their bodies as a shell, a container, or a learning device. The physical body houses that real self, like an egg shell protecting the embryo inside. Yet those who have left their bodies for a time say, "I could see the whole room," or "I could hear the doctors and nurses talking."

This tells us that the "I" which is each person's true identity isn't the physical body; it's something else, an identity inside the body, the real self.

Just as electricity and atomic energy existed long before they were discovered, so does our real self exist and many of us have not yet discovered it. These spirit beings or human identities inside our bodies come into this life to enroll into the Earth School. They bring with them, from their pre-Earth dimension two basic, defining character traits—tenderness and power.

Your real self is also extremely capable of doing all sorts of things. That's why you need to get to know your inner self. The real you is both easy to love and deserving of love. When you truly discover that spirit within, you will see how to view this whole Earth School life with all its adversity and success in an entirely different dimension. It will really become your special guide.

Anyone close to children, whose own potential realness is mostly actualizing, can see the following identity traits in a young child: wonder, awe, innocence, excitement, vitality, optimism, curiosity, teachability, resilience, playfulness, imagination, loyalty, and unconditional love. All of these combine into that marvelous spirit of youth and childhood.

The fascinating thing is you still have all of those traits that came at birth, really you do, no matter what your age.

Packed into your human self seed, then, is a very appealing identity. Can you just sense and feel that wonderful real self? Don't you long to unlock it and let it perform to its full potential. And just like any seed or sprouting tree, if it receives proper treatment to match its internal identity, the real self grows and blossoms in an unrelenting push to fulfill its high potential. Yours can become complete if you will realize what it truly is and can become.

Nothing is more vital to your completeness and happiness than fully unfolding who and what you really are.

How the Real Identity Grows

Enough proper nourishment when it is young and small, will allow your real self to grow strong and fulfill its natural identity throughout its entire emotional life. This inner-self seed is like a sparkler that needs to be lit by being held next to another brightly glowing sparkler *for as long as it takes* to ignite it.

In the same way, your self-seed can begin to grow and blossom after enough contact with another real self. Then your self-seed will continue to grow all by itself, like the already lit sparklers. This is why parents must supply each precious child with the right kind of treatment— this means love supplies that will make their self-seed grow and help that child reach his true, glowing potential.

Parents don't need to give this love in an exaggerated way. It can come in a constant, steady loving way. It will come almost entirely by personal example. Then, like a sparkler, the child's real self can go on glowing and growing and loving all by itself.

Because the real self is truly lovable and capable, it needs to be treated as a lovable, capable being in order to grow. This clearly means that parents and others need to recognize and live in their own lovable, capable inner selves in order to nurture—give spark—to their children in the proper way.

It is essential to the fulfillment of our best selves that we always be in touch with our own inner being. We are all unique individuals with our own real soul.

Think, if you will, your reaction to hearing your own name. Even though we may not have chosen it, we all like the sound of our name. It signifies us. It is our label. If you were given a word association test, what would your response be when they said, "Karen" or "Joe"—whatever your name is. Would you say, "woman," or "man," "teacher," "carpenter," "nurse?" It's simple to see that these kinds of associations identify your beautiful real self with a personal name tag, with your external roles that may or may not be truly you.

This is not wrong; even Christ was referred to at times as "the carpenter."

How much better is it if your natural responses were about your inner being with such as "beautiful spirit self," "tender and strong," "student of the Earth School," or the most exalting of all, "child of God?"

Unless parents *know* and *love* themselves—have respect, faith, and confidence in themselves—and unless they understand and thrill at their own inner identity feeling, they can't very well raise children to feel those exalted feelings. If children ever experience the real self it will have to come from some other love source and that is difficult to encounter. Yet, in a loving home, such achievement is elementary to the Earth School classroom.

In the academic world a person cannot learn chemistry from someone who doesn't understand chemistry. Could he? Similarly, you cannot give unconditional love unless you love yourself unconditionally.

When Jesus said, "Love thy neighbor as thyself," he was telling us that we cannot love our neighbor unless we love ourselves. He wasn't talking about arrogance or haughtiness or simply feeding our ego. He meant that we should have self-respect, a high opinion of our own inner being, of our own personal worth to mankind and to God who created us. The old saying, "God don't make no junk," has never been more true.

People with this quality of self-respect are not usually unreasonable, argumentative, or afraid of failing, especially with their own children. They don't need defenses such as sarcasm, permissiveness, shyness, or violence. On the contrary, they are generally understanding, firm, patient, and kind. They are self-actualizing, fulfilling their true potential and glowing from within. Understanding and loving their own true selves, they can recognize their children's real selves and nurture them with that same love.

The human feeling identity seed is quite strong and *known* to the newborn infant. The infant trusts his own inner signals from the first day of life. The child is the *sole expert* as to when to nurse, sleep, be held, and how to judge body and feeling signals. If the parents who raise this baby honor their own inner-body and feeling signals, they will automatically do the same with their baby.

Such a lucky infant that is nurtured by self-honoring parents will obey *its own body* and feeling signals, not those of someone else. If this is the case then the real self inside that child is on its way to a lifetime of happiness and decisiveness. There is so much exhilaration and joy ahead for those who have been properly nurtured to be in touch with their real self and allow it to perform to its highest level of fulfillment.

Avoid Storms

Even though each person comes into this world with the seed of a beautifully lovable and capable self, few if any of us experience perfect harmony, freedom from anxiety, and consistent, loving, firm treatment. Most parents are still learning how to be parents, so they aren't perfect at nurturing their children. That's okay.

Instead of living an ideal life, we begin to encounter problems at birth. Perhaps a tiny baby has a problem such as colic and can't digest her food very well. What happens? She cries and feels frustrated with the discomfort.

Then as a toddler, she will fall and bump her head at times. And this is just the beginning. This little girl, like everyone else, will and should encounter problems throughout her entire life because such is the nature of this life. This is to be expected. It is part of the Earth School experience.

I call this life the *Earth School of Hard Knocks*—a place where we learn by facing and overcoming difficulties. And the wonderful thing about this Earth School of hard knocks is that, at the start, each of us is given a little bag (or a big bag!) of carefully selected, custom-made problems that we have to deal with in this life.

This problem package—much like a back-pack that a child carries to school—arrives with us at birth: items such as some personality traits and the right amount of specifically selected difficulties are well packed into the package we bring.

We must, individually, overcome or conquer the bag of problems. Sooner or later the question we ask as we discover our individual problems inside that bag is, "Why? Why do I need these problems? And what is the purpose of me bringing that bag of personal challenges into this life?" These are good and appropriate questions and there are answers that we'll look at in the following pages.

It is required of all of us that we have a positive and negative force in the Earth School—conflict and harmony, good and bad, black and white—in order to grow in this life. The challenge is here for us to understand these forces and make them work for us.

A great man once said that there must be "opposition in all things." Solving these real life encounters makes our real selves grow and grow and mature into the person we ought to be. This comes when we are aware that the inner self is the student in the Earth School.

In this School, we actualize more and more of our inner potential and become more capable and more lovable as we learn to use our beautiful real selves to manage our problems. We want to make our challenges our servants. Since our problems are custom designed to strengthen our individual weaknesses, they can actually assist us by allowing and forcing us to manage them correctly. And in the process, we *grow*.

Someone said that "Every problem has a gift in hand. Solve the problem and the gift is given." Expressed another way, "No pain—no gain." We have all heard the phrase, "We must taste the bitter to prize the sweet." It's true. All these sayings show the need for adversity in our development.

Of course, with poor management of our customdesigned problems we can create additional problems for ourselves. We can fill up our lives with negative challenges and have far more suffering than we really need. Unnecessary suffering will only make our lives in the Earth School harder.

Many of us are like the sailboat owners who ignore the advice I found at the beginning of valuable manual on rough-weather sailing. We get into extra storms in life. The first sentence of the book I bought on sailing in rough waters warned: "DO NOT SEEK STORMS."

It hit me as a warning sign of life. "Avoid storms! Avoid unnecessary problems." The road signs that warn us on the highways, not only spell out the potential danger ahead, they are in designated symbolic shapes that give the very image of danger. Those internationally diamond-shaped signs catch our eye and draw us to the words, "Sharp curves, Falling rocks, Stop ahead."

The author of the sailing book in the first statements followed up his insights with this statement: "Storms will come to you all by themselves." What a commentary on real-life experiences. The author knew whereof he wrote, when he said, "DO NOT SEEK STORMS!"

Life is full of storms that will lash at you all by themselves. Keep in mind that the baggage you brought into this life with you contains all the problems you need so don't go searching for any more. Don't go looking for new ones! Also, keep your nose out of other people's problem bags. Instead, learn from solving your own bag of problems and difficulties that come to you naturally.

If you do, this will more fully actualize your true potential. When you give the challenges of life to your real self, you grow stronger and more beautiful. Trust and love your inner self more and more, then recognize and love other people's real self. In this way you get an "A" in the Earth School.

Part One
KNOW YOUR ENEMY

Chapter Two
The Substitute Self

Even though the inner self is infinitely lovable and capable, if the self-seed doesn't receive the right kind of nourishment, the kind to feed the true identity, it can't grow. In its place a *false self* grows. This is a mutation, an imitation of your true self, eclipsing the real you.

Some people see only this false self in those around them. They say, "It's a terrible thing to be human. Meanness, evil, cruelty and selfishness are everywhere." They fail to see the real human self. What they observe is a mutation, a *substitute self*—crude skills learned to survive in a sick family. Some even call it a survival self.

Mutations, Artificial, Imitations

The imitation self begins to ferment when adults treat babies or young children as if they were not innately lovable and capable. In other words, the imitation self begins to dominate and increase in strength whenever a child receives treatment that fails to match his or her true identity.

Cover-ups

The growth of a child's real self can be slowed or stunted when he or she receives unusually negative treatment. For instance, a child who is often overprotected—shielded from things that are not actually harmful—falters in developing a strong feeling of competence.

No matter how kind, nice, and helpful the parents are, the child can't develop his own abilities and discover how entirely adequate he is unless he is free to make mistakes as he tries to do as much as possible for himself. Too much "help" stunts the real self. Similarly, a child who experiences neglect, rudeness, or humiliation will feel that he is not lovable; then he won't be able to discover his innately lovable real self because others don't know it exists and can't help him nourish it.

Both the capable and lovable characteristics of the real self must be acknowledged and nurtured. When this does not happen, a false substitute self grows in place of the real self. This false self is like a layer of clouds and mist. It covers the bright sun that is like the real self (see Figure 1).

Because it originates from the feeling of *un*lovability and *in*capability, this negative self becomes a layer made of *cover-ups*: masks and games and tricks designed to "hide" what the person feels is an inferior self—not capable or lovable.

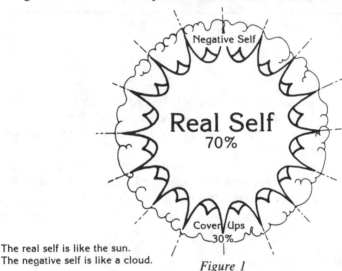

The real self is like the sun.
The negative self is like a cloud.

Figure 1

This negative self layer can be very thick or thin, depending on how much negative treatment the person has received. But almost everyone has some kind of layer of cover-ups surrounding his beautiful real self. At times, almost all of us have been treated as unlovable or incapable.

Remember that the bag of problems we all carry from birth entrance into Earth School, points up the fact that this kind of treatment is usually one of these problems. However, just as storms and bad weather test and strengthen sailors, we endure them as tests of strength of real self.

Negative treatment is not all bad unless we give up and believe the lies completely. The important point to remember is that even though the layer of cover-ups is there, the real self is also intact inside every person. It is our task to learn how to recognize the cover-ups and work through them to strengthen the real self.

Survival Self

Another way to say this is when *parents* have been abused in their own identities, they often later identify with their abusers and abuse the precious identity seed of their own children. Since an infant is mostly feelings and doesn't know anything about performances, early abuse is usually done by older siblings, teachers, friends, and parents to the innate feelings of the child.

Emotional identity abuse is done by ignoring and neglecting our feelings or worse, by *shaming* and prohibiting the expression of feelings such as crying from fear, pain, anger or giggling from joy.

A child allowed to cry for long periods of time with no attention will soon learn to dishonor and ignore, even hate, his own sacred inner feeling signals. Even more troubling, where there are domineering, needy, taking parents, the child will be forced to feel his parents feelings as if they were his own!

A child pushed in this direction over time will not be able to know who he is or what he feels. This child will live in a false self survival world like a programmed robot, without feeling, vitality, or zest for life.

Our identity seeds can be further abused with words, physical violence, and sexual taking. Words can hit as hard as fists. Sarcasm, criticism, belittling, arguing, teasing and all other forms of word put-downs and body language insults, that imply a negative identity on the part of the child, can be labeled abuse.

Physical abuse consists of such violent acts as hitting, slapping, hard squeezing, jerking, and anything like it. Any form of discipline that involves physical pain demands and gets immediate performance or external results. Regardless, such results come at a terrible price. Performance idiots love it. Some of the abuses that I see and hear of, are like "soul murder."

When we abuse others, we are burning cathedrals to fry eggs. Unfortunately, such abuse sprouts up in the next generation and continues on. Abused children will abuse their children unless the cycle is somehow broken. Just as their parents violated their precious persons, they will do the same to themselves and others with food, sex, drugs, and violence.

In the realm of abuses there are many ramifications. For example, sexual abuse has three parts at least: emotional, verbal, and physical. Treating someone as a sex object or body only denies their sacred identity as a personal or spirit being. The mentality that someone's body is more important than their spirit or their personhood is based on physical and sexual fulfillment and is identity abuse of the worst form. Unfortunately, this type of attitude abuse is rampant and proceeds all lust forms, verbal sexual harassment, or actual sexual physical contact.

These abuses abound in sick families, at work or school, wherever! They are called dysfunctional because they do not work. They are toxic or poisonous to our true human-feeling identity seed. They cause soul mutations that are formed in order to survive in an identity stifling world.

Suppose the chart—Figure 1—is a rough sketch of a woman's self layers. She has a fairly large real self compared to her cover-ups. She has experienced a good deal of positive treatment consistent from self and others with her real inner identity. For convenience, we could roughly describe her as having seventy percent real self and thirty percent negative self.

Figure 2

This person's inner sunshine can't penetrate the heavy layer of clouds surrounding it. This means that others never see this real self; all they can see are the negative survival styles used to stay alive in an identity-abusive world.

Externals Cannot Fix Internals

One of the best ways to see through the false self is to carefully notice feelings and see whether they are based on *internal* or *external* self. Such feelings as love, personal worth, and self-value originate from the real self. These feelings are based on *internal* qualities; they arise when a person is valued by himself and others purely for his humanness—when others love and cherish his beautiful inner being. There are many who become brain washed and learn to value themselves and others only on the basis of *external* things such as performances, possessions and appearances.

These people wrongly think that internal worth is directly related to externals. They think a person is worthwhile and valuable because of what he does or what he owns or looks like, not because of his innately lovable and capable inner self.

The performance externals are the things people do, such as winning awards or making all "A's" on a report card. And the *possession* externals are the things people control or own, including their physical appearance, such as size shape, looks, age, as well as such things as cars, houses, businesses, clothes, or other property. There's nothing wrong with any of these external performances or possessions; they can be of use, properly handled, as an expression of a person's beautiful real self.

But, overconcern about failure and success or physical externals, or how to get them, makes these things into counterfeits for the real self. The *way* we use our

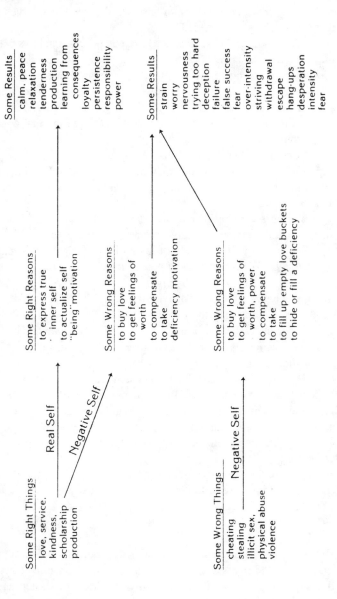

Figure 3

possessions and the *reasons* we do what we do, tell whether our feelings of self-value are based on internals or externals. In other words, they tell us which self is in charge, the real self or the substitute self.

The person whose feelings are based on internal qualities does the right thing for the right reason; he is "being motivated." That is, he does things in order to actualize his inner being, to express and celebrate his true self. His behavior will flow naturally because his real self is acting in accordance with its true nature. If this person were to help his neighbor trim a hedge, he would do it because he enjoys being with this friend and enjoys the good identity feeling that comes from caring, sharing, being outdoors, and helping.

Nonetheless, he does not give as a means of getting. It is a fact of life that a being motivated person is usually calm, peaceful and relaxed towards others. The diagram in (Figure 3) illustrates this by showing some motivations of the real self and negative self.

In contrast, many people are "deficiency motivated." The deficiency is in not knowing and loving themselves. Their substitute selves use possessions and performances to get a false feeling of lovability and capability because they believe the lie that says, "Your actions and possessions define you."

This lie leads to the really big lie that says, "There is no super lovable, super capable inner being—there is no *real* you." That is the reasoning of the substitute self. It thinks it is the only thing there is.

So when deficiency-motivated people do something like help a neighbor trim the hedge, the action has an altogether different flavor to it. It is still a "right" thing to do, but the reason has changed to "wrong."

The person who is basing his self-worth on his actions will do the right things for the wrong reasons. He'll help trim the hedge because his boss is coming to dinner the next night, and he wants the neighborhood to look good so he will look good. His reasons for acting are wrong: to *get* feelings of worth, to be approved, to compensate for feelings of inadequacy. Deficiency motivation causes overreacting and undereacting.

These come from trying too hard or too little. The negative self is in charge. The person is too intense or too laid back, and usually very tired, drained or bored. (See Figure 3.)

Deficiencies

Most of us are acting on this deficiency motivational level much of the time. We may be great teachers, architects, or physicists who inspire others, build beautiful buildings or discover great scientific truths, but often for wrong reasons. If we have any feelings of trying to get rich, trying to be somebody important, or trying to prove to ourselves that we really are OK, we have forgotten our true identities, forgotten that we *already are* somebody important. We are, in part, deficiency motivated.

A second kind of deficiency motivation is doing the wrong thing for the wrong reason. Check the diagram in Figure 3 once again. Notice that the negative self is in charge here as well. Now it has grown so large and diminished the real self so much that it thinks the way to gain acceptance and feelings of worth are to steal, cheat, lie, intimidate—in short, do whatever is required by some devious rule to create exploitation. The emotional state of many of these people is one of intensity, fear, confusion, or desperation. If this were you suffering from this state of diminished awareness of real self and if your neighbor were trimming his hedge, you'd probably wait until he took a break and steal his clippers, or worse, chop him up.

Some of us wonder why there isn't a category of wrong things for the right reasons. That is because if we are doing anything for the right reason, it is the right thing. If a nation is attacked and defends itself by going to war and killing the enemy to save itself from destruction, then it is the right thing. The people are not deficiency motivated; they are defending themselves. They must fight or be killed. The proper approach is to fight.

Obviously, doing the right thing for any reason is better than doing the wrong thing. Yet, whether a person is doing the wrong thing or the right, if it's for the wrong reason—to compensate, to get feelings of worth, to "feel better"—he will continue to feel empty because the real self cannot be nourished by externals. It simply gets more and more covered up as the negative self takes over. Usually, the more the person feels empty, the more likely he is to try to "buy" love with externals, which makes him feel the emptiness even more. So he concentrates harder on externals, hoping they will relieve the void. Often, the more the feeling of vacancy, the deeper he is sucked into the whirlpool or vicious cycle that can offer no relief.

Manifestations of emptiness that come from seeking after externals are myriad. They can be called hang-ups, psychopathology, emotional illness, and even sin. This condition is a sad mutation of the true human identity. So, what is the root cause? They are blinded to their own beauty and self-worth. In part, this is encouraged by others around them who may be suffering from the same condition, in that their human feeling identity seed has not been nourished, either.

The Lion Who Thought He was A Lamb

People who don't understand their real selves and attempt to fill their emptiness with externals remind me of the lion who thought he was a lamb.

The story goes that a lion cub was born among a herd of sheep, his mother killed, he grew up in the herd. In the process the cub was brainwashed by the sheep into thinking he was a lamb. Did they tell him this maliciously to trick him? No, they were ignorant. All they knew was how to be sheep. The fact remained that to the lion knowing how to be a lamb was garbage knowledge for him. Why? Because being a lamb didn't square with the lion's true identity. When the lion grew older, he heard this tiny voice inside his head whispering to him, "Eat the sheep." He ignored the voice. Everything he had been taught was contrary to eating sheep. "Don't eat the sheep; they are your brothers. They raised you and taught you." The two conflicting voices were his real internal self and his environmental external self. Since his external self did not match his internal self, the lion cub became very uptight. In fact, he became quite neurotic. Why? Because he believed a lie about his true identity.

When the lion goes onto the plains or jungle, what will happen? Will he be nervous? Of course he will be. Any lamb would be nervous there. It's silly, though. The lion has within himself the power to cope wonderfully with life in the jungle. That is where he belongs, but the lion has been told lies. He is scared because lambs can't survive in the jungle, everyone know that. He seeks cover-ups. This will build confidence and help him overcome fear.

What compensations can the lamb-lion turn to? Perhaps he could roar loudly all the time—like a person with a bad temper—or talk too much. Even better, he might put on a real lion skin and cover himself to fool everybody into thinking he's powerful—like a person with a superiority complex. But who would he really fool? How silly, a real lion wearing a lion skin! Why? Because he believes the lie about his identity and tries to fool himself and others with cover-ups.

This is what conceit is all about, a facade or a mockery of self-confidence. Another cover-up this lamb-lion could use is shyness. He could withdraw and never go into the jungle at all, or hide every time something scary came by. Perhaps he could take some type of magic pills that would make him feel big and strong, or would help him forget the jungle entirely. He could become sexually involved to show that he is attractive and wanted. All these tricks are efforts to prove to himself who he is, because he doesn't know.

Many people travel life with an experience similar to the lion. Children are often brainwashed by constantly being shamed and put down. They are taught that they're dumb and that their opinions and feelings have no value. In other words, that they are unlovable and incapable. Just like the lion whose inner self kept resisting the lie that he was a lamb, kids will fight the lie as hard as they can.

But the struggle is difficult. Too often the lie finally wins and the child gives up his true inner identity because this is the easiest way to gain at least a little acceptance (this is misinterpreted as love) from parents and others who are unconsciously doing the brainwashing. The child is buying "love" at the price of his own identity. Pretty high price. This is survival in a sick world where the human feeling identity seed is abused.

Not everyone is as confused as the lamb-lion. Contrast him with a man whom a friend of mine met at a conference and party in London long ago. My friend saw a lot of people there who didn't understand their true internal identities: they were using "crutches" such as drinking, smoking, and seduction to get love substitutes. But my friend did notice one man who wasn't doing these self-abusive acts. He asked the man why he wasn't participating with the others. The man drew himself up straight and tall and said, "I'm from royal parents. Nobility tries not do such things." (It was true, then.)

This nobleman knew something about himself that kept him from needing to lower himself to use such love substitutes. In a way, any person who recognizes his true identity will feel as this true nobleman. All spirit selves are noble, and they all want to act nobly and to be treated nobly.

Three Inner Layers, A Summary

The poor lamb-lion story shows how the spirit self cannot grow properly without nourishment that matches its true inner identity. Without this nourishment, phony cover-ups grow instead of protecting the person from the pain of insistent, negative treatment which says, "You are not lovable and not capable." This layer of pain builds up to surround and smother the real self. And then, to cover up the pain, a substitute self grows. So instead of two layers, as in Figures 1 and 2, we really have three inner layers when we count the pain layer between the real self and the substitute self, as shown in Figure 4.

• **The real self or human feeling identity seed.** The spirit self, or heavenly being inside the body, is very positive. Often, however, it is small because of inadequate nourishment and mutates to the false self.

• **The Pain layer.** The primary lie is formed because of negative treatment, treatment which teaches us that we are not good or lovable, not capable. This treatment comes from the negative selves of parents and others who do not recognize their own true identities. Many patients call the pain layer their garbage pile.

• **The layer of cover-ups.** Games, styles, or psychological defenses form over the pain layer. These games or styles consist of externals used as substitutes. The external cover-ups are the tricks, the "lion skins," that people use to cover up the pain of the lies they learned in their childhood. These games are the *secondary lies.* They say, "Let's pretend that we are the greatest, the shyest, or the sexiest. "But just like the lamb-lion, why do we need to pretend if we already are lovable and capable? Who do we think we are fooling? What we need to do instead is to get to know our real self, to discover our true identity by loving the wounded child of the past who is hurting, angry, scared, and needs good love.

The Freedom of Truth

Knowing and feeling the truth about both selves keeps us safe forever more from this old kind of pain. If someone does not like us, we can immediately ask, "Which of his selves is talking?" And which self of mine is he talking about?"

A real self always likes another real self, that is part of its nature. So only a negative self dislikes a real self. A negative self will usually not like another negative self either, because they clash and compete—both are taking.

The only exception to this occurs when two negative styles are symbiotic, meaning they are opposites but fit together like a domineering man and a timid, appeasing woman, or a too helpful woman and an insecure man.

The Substitute Self

Pain Layer

Real Self

Early Negative Treatment

Hang Ups
Cover Ups
Games

Figure 4

A negative self is usually uncomfortable around a real self and so does not like it. Sometimes., a negative self doesn't like very much at all; it is miserable and wants everyone else to feel the same way.

To repeat, a real self always likes another real self, but does not like a false or negative self. However, unlike a negative self, a real self is intensely interested in helping because real selves are naturally helpful and encouraging. A real self can see the potential for self actualization beneath another person's false self and will tolerate a negative self temporarily for the sake of that potential nourishment. But real selves are not pleasers to buy love. They know and honor their own sacred feelings, not others' feelings to buy their love. In this way those who take prostitute their sacred identity for a little fake love. And also, real selves don't marry false selves. Like marry like. Rescuing someone by marriage is very sick and is only done by two mostly false selves.

So if someone doesn't like you and you are mostly in your real self, you will say (to yourself), "They are in their false self right now. It is an honor to be their enemy."

To summarize then, we can see that all interactions beginning with any two people have to be one of the following types:

Type I (mostly in) Real Self to Real Self
Type II (mostly in) Real Self to False Self
Type III (mostly in, False Self to False Self

Type I is the highest, the best, the most fun and the one to which we all aspire. It is love, human family love. It is the foundation of all other forms of love: parent to child, friend-to-friend, romantic, man to God, and all those relations we hold dear.

Type II interactions are supposed to be helping situations where one person, because of emotional wounds of some kind, is now in their false survival self and the other person stays in the positive. The next chapter will describe in more detail some of the common styles the negative self can take in an attempt to survive childhood identity abuse or poor love supplies.

In a Type II interaction, the one remaining *mostly*—and this is the key—in their real self wants to help the damaged person back to their real self. This is done by offering the "weird person" his favorite love supplies, not substitutes. If this is done genuinely and the mostly negative person receives that love supply, the two people can once again enjoy a Type I interaction, real-to-real.

Sometimes a "wound," like a phobia, will be so severe that the real self cannot get the false self out. Often the mostly real self person can be dragged down into his negative self. His wounds also have now been threatened and his false self styles from childhood will go into action. We then see the overreactions and underreactions (shown in figure 5, page 20). This is a Type III interaction.

In Type III interactions we have two subtypes or kinds. They are two forms of negative-to-negative interaction.

a. Symbiotic. Like a submissive wife married to a domineering man. Both need the other's negative style to complement their negative style. This is a lot like bees needing flowers and flowers needing bees.

b. Anti-symbiotic. Here are two similar styles that clash, like two domineering people who mostly fight and argue.

When we realize we are in a Type III interaction with someone, we need "time out," NOW!

Never stay in a mess like that for long. Go to your "room" or some other previously agreed upon place to get some space. One married man said to me, "I determined never to raise my voice to my wife. If I'm about to do so, I will go outside immediately. As a result, I have spent much of my married life out-of-doors."

What do you do when you have that space? Remember, you are alone with your negative self. There are many excellent ways to get back into your real self. You can do it alone or ask help from someone of your choice. The person you call on must be mostly in his Real Self as outlined in the chapter on love supplies from others and love supplies from yourself. See chapters five and seven. Here is a chart to show the three types of interaction and their movements as shown by arrows and giving the favorite love supplies (FLS).

Type I: Real Self to Real Self (Love)

↑ then

Type II: Real Self to False Self (Help)

↑ then —→ F.L.S. given

Type III: False Self to False Self (Time out)

    (a) symbiotic

    (b) anti-symbiotic

(Arrows show the way back to Type I.)

Understanding which type of interaction we are in and *saying it out loud to our partner* is an amazing power that can help so much to get us back to Type I. Even if we are in Type III and have to yell or scream, "I'm being weird! I need space!" This is better than staying and fighting.

Some of the greatest wounds and meanest things we have ever said or done have been so because we stayed in Type III with a loved one, when we should have left. We didn't mean it, but it can sting like anything and never be forgotten by a dear partner, friend, or child.

Giving a favorite love supply to help another move from Type II to Type I is also extremely helpful and often a great surprise to us. Many spouses, children, parents, and friends *don't even know* the other one's favorite love supply and so are helpless when they get into Type II. Be sure to tell your children, spouse, and others what helps you the most when you are wounded. If it isn't in the chart (see page 75), make up a new one. (Be sure it isn't an external to fix and internal, such as food, sex, drugs, money, orderliness, escape, fame, performance or a hundred other externals.)

Chapter Three
Some Styles of
the False Self

Sources of the False Self

$\mathbf{Y}$ou can't fight an enemy you can't see, especially one that you don't recognize as your enemy. Not only that, you must understand an enemy if you are going to destroy him. All good generals, football coaches, and administrators of anything know that they must study their opponents' strategies and tactics so well that they can predict their plans and be ready to defeat them.

That's why it's important to learn about negative styles, so you can recognize your negative self coming out and get back into your real self as soon as possible. The more you know about your false-self styles, the more easily you can learn to control your negative self and encourage your real self to grow.

This idea contradicts what some people say. I call these views *Pollyanna positivism*. They say that we should not think about false survival selves. Rather, we should think positive thoughts all the time. If a negative thought comes into your mind, you are not supposed to analyze its source; just throw it out and replace it with a positive thought. Sometimes patients have even complained that the new positive replacement like "singing a happy tune" now triggers off the old negative thought! The reality is that quickly eliminating a negative thought by replacing it with a positive one doesn't give the best permanent solution. It is hurriedly shoving the negative aside without defeating it.

Weaknesses cannot be changed into strengths by merely pushing them aside. The *causes* have to be dealt with and understood, then conquered. You have to confront your negative environment with determination. Like generals, coaches, and managers, you need to understand your opponents—and your own negative-self style—in order to gain the advantage over those forces. Knowledge is power, and ignorance is helplessness.

So let's talk about some of the tricks and cover-ups that the false self uses to compensate for the pain of feeling less than good enough.

There are two basic survival self styles, and both are extremes of behavior. One is to *overreact*. This is an aggressive, domineering style. The other is to *underreact*. This is a passive style. For short, we call these styles *overs* and *unders*. Most people have a preferred style.

For instance, when I'm in my negative, I usually use *overs* to try and get what I want. After a while, if that fails to work, I may switch to *unders*. Some people stick exclusively to one style, whether it gets them what they want or not. It is usually what worked best in their childhood.

Here are examples of these two false self styles. *Overs* include things like yelling and screaming, violence, sarcasm, superiority, bossiness, bragging, perfectionist, workaholic, and overcontrol of others. *Unders* include things like withdrawing or escaping from situations; being quiet, shy and fake meek; pouting; being a doormat; pleaser; and some depressions. The unders are often submissive to what others want, even if it hurts them.

These negative self characteristics develop and divide into overs and unders style types. Notice that overs are usually aggressive and controlling, while unders are passive and self-punishing. Certain other negative self cover-ups and games can result from either an overs or an unders style. These may be manifested in selfishness, drug abuse, sex abuse, over-eating, and a host of other carnal outlets. *Acting out* on others or *acting in on yourself* fail to completely describe all the lies and tricks of the false survival self, though they are a good general way to characterize our weird self styles.

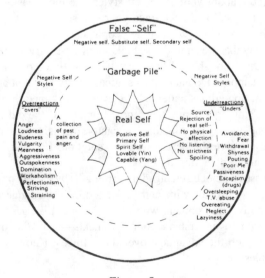

Figure 5

In order to understand our false selves better, let's look at some of the most common negative cover-ups we copy and create. Most of these can be expressed as either overs or unders, depending on the style of the person (which helped them survive in their childhood dysfunctional home).

Temper

Temper is a common negative style. Almost everybody uses it; it's a real favorite. It is an overreaction like yelling, loud screaming, hitting, sobbing, or "speeding." Temper risks being out of control, which means a person often says things that he does not mean.

Temper can be expressed through an unders style as well. All the person has to do is pout, look mad, or refuse to speak. Angry silence is the unders temper in action. And lots of people find this negative style most useful for getting their way. It has also been called passive aggression.

The little baby expects *so much* love, attention, and help. When attention does not come immediately and the baby needs food, changing, holding or whatever, it cries. It should cry. It believes it is lovable and deserves immediate and accurate love supplies.

Crying is good. It implies self-love and respect for one's needs. It is the sign of intense feeling. This is why, when the baby doesn't get the help he believes he deserves, he screams. This is good anger, however. It is expressing identity frustration.

Please keep this in mind; it is a rule of mine: *All children's feelings are good and should be honored,* but not always obeyed, yet deeply understood and validated. In other words, honor negative and positive feelings, but obey only positives.

Crying will not spoil the child, but rather validate his precious feeling identity. But if these demands of the baby's frustrate the parents, the baby may learn to use anger negatively. Good anger is a defense and a protection against felt danger.

One of the most convincing substitutes for a genuine feeling of capability is a feeling of external control, a feeling of power over others. If you don't feel that you are truly lovable and cable, at least you can get some comfort out of feeling powerful. That's one way anger may become a *love substitute,* a phoney payoff. Often people will say, "I like my temper because it puts me in control," or "I want to get control of others before they get control of me, so I get angry." Maybe they feel weak and able to be controlled.

When Eric returned to school after summer vacation, he noticed that his teacher's hair was a different color than it had been the year before. He looked at her skin; then he looked at her hair and finally blurted out, "Miss Jones, your skin doesn't match your hair."

"What? she asked with a hostile voice.

"You have the skin of one person and the hair of another," he said. He kept looking at her face and then her hair. "You have 'plastic' hair."

She started to turn red. Her neck became blotchy and the blotchiness started to spread to her face. Finally she spoke with a tremor in her voice, "There isn't any set hair color for a certain skin tone."

He wasn't listening to her rebuttal and went right on to say, "You don't have it together."

Eric might as well have said that she was not congruent on the outside; how can she be congruent on the inside? This upset her.

She became more and more angry with Eric. In desperation she screamed at him, "You go over in that corner and sit down on the floor where the stupid kids sit!"

He did as he was told. But as he walked to the corner he mumbled, "I might be sitting down on the outside, but on the inside I'm standing up straight and tall." With that she got even more upset and referred him to me, the school psychologist.

In the psychologist's office Eric said, "Mr. Ellsworth, her skin doesn't match her hair, does it?"

"No, it doesn't. You're right, Eric. But it hurts her feelings when you confront her that way."

Later when I saw the teacher, she said in defense of her new appearance, "This summer I looked in the mirror and saw all the gray hairs sprouting. (She believed the lie that her worth depended on her appearance; this was her pain.) "I got scared," she said. "You know, Sterling, I'm getting old. I know that young bodies get more 'love' than old bodies." That was a strange comment that depends on the observer. Older people may get a great deal more *real* love supplies than young people do from healthy people. Nonetheless, I advised her that it was not real love; it was a substitute love supply that she was experiencing, conditional on her hair color.

She went on, "But I thought that since I'm looking older, I would dye my hair black and look younger."

Did it work? Of course not. What she had done was try to cover one lie with another, the lie that young is better than old. It can't possibly be overcome by the second lie, which was "I have black hair, not gray, any more." So it was that Eric's observation got into her wound where her pain resided. Eric also had a wound or he would have been more kind, considerate, and tactful.

No one can cause you to lose your temper unless they have something you want (or think you want). If you believe they have it, whether they do or not, it can frustrate you, and make you angry. But *you do it* to yourself by your frustrated, dependent expectations.

What people most often want from others is approval or acceptance in some form. They want to be reassured that they are *lovable* and *capable*, because they don't know that for certain. That was Eric's teacher's problem. She wanted the children and others to like and respect her, and she thought they wouldn't unless she looked young.

But the truth is that if you want someone's approval that badly, you are looking for a love need that should have been filled when you were young. It was the job of your parents. They were to make you feel loved and capable so that you would grow up with positive feelings about yourself. If you will look deep, you will see that when you are hurt or sad, it's because you are believing a lie about yourself. You can't see your beautiful real self through the mist and clouds of the pain layer that surrounds it. You do have these layers around your real self.

When you get angry, somebody has uncovered your pain layer. An angry person is a suffering person. You need love supplies from your big, good self for the little wounded child within, which helps you not to need love from others.

Temper is usually just one reaction to the pain of not getting approval or acceptance. But the thing to remember is that such conditional approval isn't always the real thing. It just isn't. It can't fill the void left over from childhood of an undernourished real self. Instead, we need to recognize the unconditional real need and get it filled, as we will understand later.

Benjamin Franklin said that you can measure the size of a person by the size of the things that make him mad. What does it take to make you angry? What is it that other people have that you want? What are your wounds? What are the things that you don't want anyone to say or do to you?

Managing Temper Correctly Can Make It Go Away

Your negative self will try to convince you that it is better to be angry than to cry. You may already believe this. Your real self, however, doesn't need temper to cover up its feelings. Your real self likes true expression and out-front feelings. Anger is never the deepest feeling we have; it is a secondary expression triggered by underlying sadness and hurt. And the hurt is caused by frustrated expectations that most people will love you just the way you are.

Lie/Expectation → Sadness/Hurt → Temper

So, when you are angry, what should you do? The first rule is to get off by yourself, if you can, and express this anger safely. If you can do it silently, then finish sentences to yourself such as, "I'm mad because. . . " Say it ten times at least. If you are in private, you can put a pillow in a chair and pretend it is the person's false self you are angry with. Yell, scream, hit if you have to. Hit the pillow. Hit it hard. But *never* the person you are angry with, especially a child.

All primary feelings are good and should be honored in yourself by expressing them honestly and safely, which is usually alone. This is less harmful since anger is created by our false self. You can also finish sentences out loud if you are alone. Try it. It works. Confronting people in person usually backfires, especially if they are in their negative self.

If you do inner-child work, you can go back in time and say to your child of the past, "Has anything like this ever happened to us before?" If you are in touch with your little inner child, he may show you a repeat of the past. So much of our false self is copied from our parents' styles. The false self is a collection of survival skills we thought we needed at the time to cope with an abusive, or an otherwise dysfunctional family.

Don't beat yourself up because your false self ran your body for a while. It is a learning experience that is necessary so you won't die dumb and get an "F" in Earth School.

After you've done this first feeling step, you can move on to step two, which is more cognitive, or in your head. The second rule is, "Don't focus on what someone *else* is doing. If a rattlesnake bites you, should you go racing off into the bushes looking for the snake, shouting, "I'm going to kill you if it's the last thing I do!" That will be the last thing you do. Why? Because you already have the poison inside you and it spreads. Killing the snake at that very moment ought to be the least of your concerns. It's time to concentrate on getting that poison out. So forget about the snake. If you worry about the snake, you'll lose your life.

In the same way, when you're angry you've got poison inside you. Strangely, many will concentrate on chasing after the "snake" that made them upset. Don't do it. It will only make the poison circulate faster throughout your body, and you'll hurt your inner self even more and maybe someone else, too.

If someone has hurt your feelings, dug into your wound, uncovered your pain layer, and made you angry, what should you do? Forget the other person, and concentrate on getting the poison out of you by analyzing your feelings and the inner layer they ooze from. When you feel anger, ask yourself what the hurting feelings beneath this anger really are. What triggers the anger? Then ask, "What is the lie that triggered the hurt? What negative lies am I believing about myself?" What false expectation did I have? If you know what the lies are, you can dump them.

Eric's teacher could have figured out that her hurt feelings were because Eric pointed out her cover-up (her black hair) and implied that she was a phony. And the lie that triggered the hurt is that she is too old to be loved and respected. She believes her worth is partly determined by her age and appearance. And she expected people to go for it. Now she could ask some more questions:

What is my cover-up?
What does he have that I think I want? (Expectation)
Do I really need that from him, and are my definitions of need exaggerated
and co-dependent? (most important)
Does he really have what I want?

If she were honest with herself, Eric's teacher might answer these questions something like this:

What is my cover up?
Black hair, which makes me feel younger, and more worthwhile.

What does he have that I want?
Approval and acceptance, of me and of my new young facade.

Do I really want that from him?
I don't really need him to like me or my fake hair color.
This has nothing to do with my real self or his.

Is he in his real self and does he really have what I want?
No. His false self doesn't determine my worth. I am already lovable and
capable. His real self already loves me, if he is in his real self.

By answering these questions, you can help keep the temper poison from destroying your awareness of reality. Also, you can learn to be more honest and deeply understanding. But besides answering these questions, you must understand the people who hurt you. Forgive yourself for being so mixed up and co-dependent on them that you are vulnerable to their hurt.

If you don't gain this insight, hate collects and festers inside you as surely as snake poison; you pile up grudges and carry them around as a burden all the time. Have you ever seen people who live with hate? They are filled with poison. Such people have heavy lines on their dark, hard faces. They rarely smile, laugh, sing, or whistle. Hatred rules their lives like Scrooge. It extinguishes the light in an otherwise radiant face. Their children and friends, if they have any, may have poison spilled all over them as well, and it can infect them. Is it worth it?

We don't get mad unless another person has something we think we want, or unless someone uncovers our pain layer or gets into our childhood wounds. Some of these may have scabbed over, but we let someone dig open the scab. We will learn how to fix our wounds in Chapter Seven, so no one can dig into them.

The more a person has love supplies (or substitutes) we want, the more angry, hurt, and impatient we become. We can call these people "major expectation sources." (M.E.S.S.). Think of the person who can get you the maddest, the fastest and for the longest time. What does he or she have that you want, and how much? If this person has your whole worth, your identity, your purpose and meaning, all your love supplies, you are in deep, deep trouble. Your co-dependency on that person is huge.

There is all need there and no love. Who are these major expectation sources? Usually they turn out to be spouses, lovers, children, bosses, dearest friends, partners, parents, and others of a similar nature. You know yours and you know what is best for you to do about the situation. Wait for feelings to come first. When it is time you will "get your eggs out of their basket," fix your expector, and get what you want from yourself or God. "No one has anything I want; everything I want is in my own heart."

Now there is also a good kind of anger. There is such a thing as *firmness*. We were not created doormats or jellyfish. Resolve and firmness come from the real self and don't resemble temper at all. They express tough love instead of trying to conceal or compensate for feelings of inadequacy. Firmness will be discussed in detail later under **Love Supplies from Others**.

Impatience

Impatience is another common style of the substitute self. The impatient person doesn't know his real self very well. He doesn't know he is lovable and capable. And since he feels incapable, he is usually afraid that he won't be able to achieve his desired goals (often exaggerated in importance). He doesn't trust himself deep down, so he can't trust others. This causes fright, insecurity, and unsureness. It actually makes the person want to rush at everything he does. The person who trusts his beautiful self and believes people are lovable and capable can demonstrate patience and ease. This person has faith in his own real abilities.

Just like temper, impatience can be expressed as part of an overs or an unders style. Both overs and unders impatient people carry a sense of urgency or intensity about them, though they may express it differently. Notice how impatient people clench their jaw and speak harshly when things don't go right? Hitler had this style and mannerism about him.

Distrusting his lovable and capable self, he doesn't believe that he has the time to slow down, to calm himself. If he slows down, he may not get all that he wants. If your favorite negative style is overs, your negative self probably tries too hard and hurries too quickly in an anxious, worrisome way. It may exhibit temper. Its basic message is "Do it! Grab it now! If you don't get it now, you won't get it at all! Strive and strain and ruin your brain."

Such a person is tense under pressure because he is so impatient and worried.

Some with an unders style of impatience carry the same intensity, but in a quiet worrisome inner way. This person usually has an anxious look and probably has headaches; he may even have ulcers. Distrusting his own and others' adequacy, he believes that people can't take care of their own needs, handle their own problems or cope with unusual situations.

This gives him a great deal to worry about. "Will Johnny be all right climbing on those rocks? Can Suzie really handle taking care of a toddler all day by herself?" These people are often overprotective. They have to be, because they don't believe that anyone is truly capable, even themselves. The sad thing is that their children and others whom they worry over may believe the lie that they are inadequate. Johnny thinks that he must not be capable of climbing safely and exploring on his own, because his mother doesn't think he can. There goes a little ray of Johnny's real self. It is lost behind a cloud of lies.

Both kinds of people, the unders and the overs, distrust and ignore their own abilities and preciousness because they don't know how capable and lovable they really are.

Sometimes these feelings of distrust reach the point of desperation. At that point, a person's *wants* become desperate *needs*. (The entertainment and advertising industries recognize and play upon this quality in people. There's nothing advertisers like better than a basically distrustful, impatient person who's quick to follow every fad, fearing that he or she may get behind and miss out.)

By contrast, healthy people who know their real selves to be extremely capable and adequate and who know their children have the same kind of real selves, will trust themselves and others. They will also assess situations realistically instead of overprotecting. In the case of Johnny's mother, she will help him climb on things that are suited to his ability while he is very young, even though he many still take an occasional tumble. As he gets older, she'll make sure he knows how to climb on rocks safely, then trust his ability to care for himself.

Suppose she has an older son who is late riding home on his bike on a dark night without a bicycle light. She might worry a little about the lack of lighting, but her real self will say, "I think he will make it. He is usually careful. He knows he doesn't have a light." (No doubt the next day she will take him to buy a light for his bike). That is a healthy separating of the boy's real self from his external actions. That is trusting the self to cope with the situation.

A healthy person like this mother has time to slow down. She doesn't feel compelled to rush from one thing to another because she trusts her beautiful real self to do the things that need to be done. She has the time to talk, to listen, and to get her work done calmly. At the same time, she won't over trust, such as letting her child play jacks in the middle of a busy street, or allowing her boy to ride in the dark without his light.

Parents need to protect their children from danger, but if they believe in their own innate adequacy, they will be more trusting and less impatient with others.

Poor Parenting—a Lack of Love Supplies

One result of living in our false self is poor parenting. This term is too general to convey a very clear picture, but you'll see what I mean as I discuss the unders and the overs style used by parents who don't know about their own real selves. These are only *a few* examples of poor parenting.

What are the indications that describe the different kinds of poor parenting? Well, one is *neglect.* That's an easy one to name because everyone knows that children need attention and love from their parents if they are to develop that identity seed normally. When they are left alone too much or abandoned, they usually develop severe problems. The neglectful parent is an example of an unders style of parenting. Since this person doesn't know about the beautiful real self inside, he or she *underacts* to the challenges of parenthood and doesn't do enough, perhaps wanting out altogether. The kids get sent to camp all summer, maybe to boarding school during the winter, or else out onto the street as soon as they get home from school. Then there are those who are left with a baby sitter most of the time. And what about the latch-key kids?

In every case, the child sees very little of his parents. In extreme cases, they are abandoned and have to be placed in foster homes. It's easy to see why a child would assume he was unlovable if his father or mother walked out and left him, either physically or emotionally. Often this happens because parents are love starved themselves and are always gone, finding their love substitutes in their work or social life.

These neglectful parents don't use their children to gain a substitute feeling of lovability and capability. They would rather forget about their children and turn to other cover-ups to fill their emptiness. For instance, they may concentrate on achieving great success in their careers; on special hobbies, service, or political work; or they may choose random sexual encounters or alcoholism to cover up their pain.

There are many other styles of unders besides neglect in parenting. Some others are doing "poor me" with their kids, trying to get them to fill their empty love buckets by making them feel sorry for their parents. Making them feel guilty is another way. Blaming them for our misery, our pain, our divorce—is poisonous to their human feeling identity-seed.

The silent treatment is another horrible way to make children feel shame, abandonment, and terror. Never do this to any child. Rather, tell them you are angry, sad, unhappy, just upset. Even if you have to scream or yell such things as, "I am in my bad self and it's not *your* fault! This type of action would be a thousand times better than silence and body language which horribly shames their identity as loving beings.

Being shy, withdrawn from life, being depressed all the time, in denial, or hiding from the truth or from trial and error in our lives and our growth, are all unders styles and will poison our children as they have poisoned us.

Another example of poor parenting by unders is the pleaser/doormat/caretaker style. When children are used for our love sources and we please our false selves to buy their love, we have destroyed ourselves as parents. Being too permissive and too weak as parents, holding our feelings in, spoiling our children so they will like us, is not love. This is giving in order to get. We end up taking and pleasing the child for our unmet needs.

Though the child seems to enjoy our giving, underneath hostility grows, and often we are amazed to feel their contempt for us. When we hear their voice tone and see their facial expression, especially in teens, we know that we have lost. Some parents try to be nice to their children in order to please, but the children see through it. It does not *flow* from the self love and happiness of the parent.

The overs style of parents is what I call a *super parent*. The super parent seldom knows he has great internal worth, (from negative treatment in the past which surrounds his beautiful real self and blocks out much of its light). True to form, this parent looks around for a substitute by asking, "What can I do to prove to *myself* and to others that I'm a good, worthwhile person?" These actions are not unlike the lion who wanted to prove he was tough enough for the jungle. And then the parent sees his little children, looking confidently back at him, anxious to please and eager to love and be loved. He can hardly resist using the child to cover up his pain and fill his own empty love bucket.

The strategy of super parents is also to give in order to get. They want their children to have a good, positive experience, but they also desperately need to feel that they themselves are good parents and good people. They are out to "prove" this. So much of their giving has strings attached. Almost everything they give, whether money, clothes, toys, cars, hugs, advice, or attention has a price tag which the parent attaches to the item. This is not really a gift to the child; rather, it is a sale or exchange. They might as well say, "I'll give you something, and you give me something." And the bargaining goes on. True love is never bargaining.

Things usually go well for these super parents *as long as* the child cooperates and gives back what the parent wants. Needless to say, the children are very good at sensing when they are being manipulated. Most, sooner or later, refuse to play the game. At that point, super parents, who so much want the approval and good opinion of their children, lose out completely. They often get rejection and loneliness, hostility and resentment from their kids.

What are some of the ways parents give in order to get this substitute feeling of worth? There are many ways. I have listed three categories to show how they accomplish this:

1. Those who get their worth from children's performances.

2. Those who give their children too much money and too many possessions in order to convince themselves that they are good parents.

3. Those who get their feelings of worth by sacrificing their personal interests and activities and doing everything for their children.

Performance-crazy Super Parents

The first type of super parent over-values external performance and usually has high expectations. This method doesn't work unless the children are able to perform well. So many parents of high intellect, with competitive children, use this to their ends. When their children do well or achieve some special honor, they get the payoff which amounts to a reassurance to them that they are good parents. They say to themselves, "Look what Mark did. Now, everyone can see the proof of how capable I am as a parent. And since I'm his father or mother, it's obvious that I must be a good parent."

This type of parent will attend every single event that his child participates in at school, church, or the community in a concerted effort to hear the praise. How could he miss one of these where he can grandstand? Mark might do something that would reflect well on Mom and Dad. This type of parent is like the mother of the fourteen-year-old boy who told me, "When I was in the sixth grade, I ran the 50-yard dash and won a blue ribbon. I brought it home from school and said, 'Look, Mom. I won a blue ribbon!' I barely had the words out of my mouth before she snatched the ribbon out of my hand and ran next door to show Mable, shouting, 'Mable, Mable, look! My son won a blue ribbon!'"

Everything this boy did his mother snatched up and stuffed into her empty love bucket.

This could be the same woman who said after a year or two of marriage, "I hate marriage. It is not at all like the movies. What am I going to do?" Then it dawns on her. "I know. I'll have a baby. That will end my misery." Fourteen years later, that baby is still being used to give her love supplies. She smothers him. And what will be the natural result? Hateful or passive rejection and rebellion by the child, often manifesting itself in the teen years.

Over-giving Super Parents

The second type of super parent tries to *buy* love from his kids by giving them material things. This is the parent who always has his wallet open—Frank the bank. His kids receive new cars as Christmas presents; or if he can't afford cars, the very best bicycles, musical instruments, or sports equipment. This parent thinks money can buy admiration, respect, and love, but it is obvious to the children that they are being bribed. They usually turn out to be extremely spoiled, demanding, and greedy adults.

Isn't it sad that these parents have not experienced enough of themselves to know that their children would naturally love and respect the parents' real selves without any buying, if the kids could only *see* and *feel* their real selves?

A survey of about two hundred children clearly demonstrated that material things are not what children really want. This group of children was asked to complete the sentence, "I like my daddy because . . ."

What was the answer in most cases? There wasn't one child who wrote, "He gives us lots of clothes, nice car, a plastic something or other." All said, "I like my daddy because he plays with me." And such things as "He takes me on hikes," or "He listens to me."

These fathers are giving of themselves. It's really true that children usually don't feel close to their parents because of their open pocketbooks or all their hours of work. They love and appreciate their parents for the real love given: the time unselfishly offered out of the parent's life to do little things that count. Sometimes just wrestling on the floor, playing some game, or reading a story. These activities are important. They remember this type of love with no strings attached.

I remember one mother who didn't understand this kind of love at all. She thought she could buy her son the career she wanted for him (something a good many parents attempt). She told me, "All I ever wanted was to have John be a medical doctor."

"But, Mrs. Arnold, he doesn't want to be a doctor," I said. "He hates medicine as a career." He had confided his feelings to me.

"But I want him to be a doctor," she said, and she started to cry.

I flatly told her, "That is a selfish attitude."

"Why is it selfish? I am paying for his degree. I should be able to buy what I pay for."

She might as well have said, "I purchased a boat; I should get a boat. I can purchase a doctor . . . ."

"That's crazy," I said. "He isn't some object. He's a person with a life of his own."

She cried some more.

"I know it hurts you and makes you cry not to have what you always wanted," I said.

Then she said, "I don't want to be old and die without a doctor that I can trust."

This mother was using her son to keep her safe from the thing she feared. She figured if she paid the price, he would give her what she wanted. The son went to medical school and flunked out. He tried to please her, but his interest was not there.

Contrast this with the father who sent his son to college with $700 to pay his tuition. The son saw a beautiful guitar for sale in a store window for that price; and since he enjoyed playing guitar and always had to borrow one to play, he bought the one in the window. It took all the money.

That weekend he went home, expecting to get another $700 from his father. He tried by promising to earn the money and pay it back. He reminded his father how hard it would be for him to get an education without the money. He needed to eat as well. The father gave good advice and no money when he said, "When you're hungry, lick the back of your guitar."

The father had enough money to buy the entire music store and some left over, but he recognized this as a learning experience for his son. Later the son got a job as a janitor cleaning out classrooms, going hungry part of the time, but his father loved him. This father loved his son enough to give him assertiveness and let him experience his own natural consequences.

This is real love if he wasn't mean or angry. His long-term reward will be genuine love and respect from his son and, perhaps, a wealthy son. At least the son learned the value of money, unlike so many children of wealthy parents.

Sacrificing Super Parents

The third type of super parent gives up all claims to a life of his own and lives his life almost entirely through and for his children. Such parents usually sacrifice their personal interests and recreation for their children and often do everything for them. They may say such things as, "We would never leave our kids with a baby sitter." Things such as homework, paper routes, chores, and household tasks are not part of these children's lives. This super mom would rather clean the bathroom herself than teach her children to do it. "It is easier, and it's cleaner if I do it," the mother will say. "Besides, the kids will be happier and they'll like me more."

The truth is, they will take advantage of her more, see her more as their servant, and therefore respect her less. They will not love her as much as if she let her real self handle the jobs of life and taught her children to be more responsible.

Because these parents' entire lives revolve around their children, they are more obviously dependent on their children than any other super parents. When the children grow up and get more involved in school activities and other interests, and especially when they leave home, these parents often crash. Some of these mothers have nervous breakdowns because their lives have lost all meaning and purpose. It's true what they say. Their hobby has been eliminated. Many of these women (it tends to be women instead of men) discover that they don't like or even know their husbands; they have been too engrossed in their children to pay much attention to the man around the house. That's one reason many divorce at this stage in their lives. This has been called "empty nest syndrome."

Such parents will expect their grown children to call regularly, and will become upset when they don't. And why don't they? Because even if they were able to surprise mom or dad with a phone call instead of feeling that it was expected, parents would take, take, take. These parents want to use this as proof of love to cover up their pain. This kind of super dad or mom will say the kids are "ungrateful," then say, "Don't they realize all we did for them?" Of course they don't. None of it was really freely given for *them.*

These super parents were taking all the time in order to get, and the strange thing about it is they will deny ever having done such a thing.

Often children of these parents will say, "I was my mother's mother; I feel as if I raised her." They are forced to be adults at age eight and made to feel guilty if mom is sad. They get the idea that they are somehow in charge of mommy's feelings and emotions. And they are; that is the irony of the whole thing. They were soul murdered. They couldn't feel their own feelings. They had to feel their mom's feelings and be her caretaker and she was theirs!

Also, they sense that their mother has given herself up in favor of her child's performance. The responsibility is too great to unload on a child. Resentment and, at times, open hostility erupt. The child has every right to feel hurt and anger; that very real person has been robbed of a childhood with a healthy upbringing.

When parents don't know their real selves or try to get a false feeling of lovability and capability from their children, they fool themselves. They can't get in touch with their real selves by using their kids as cover-ups. Instead, they become dependent on their children and they are vulnerable to them. If the children behave badly, the parents feel that they themselves are somehow bad. If the children perform well, the parents feel successful.

The irony of the super parents' situation is that *they drive their children away* by trying to get from them something (love) which the parents already have covered up inside themselves. Their children often ignore them in their old age. This is the very thing they want for that child to come and fill them up. They are left love starved. How miserable old age can be in such loneliness!

If only those parents had foresight to prevent such sad results. If they would look inside and see it was done to them and heal it, then they could discover their own beautiful selves and become givers instead of takers. And the sooner the better.

Parenting, like marriage, is a relationship that requires giving, not taking. It offers a chance to serve, not to be served. If your love bucket is empty because your real self is all covered up, you won't be happy being a marriage partner, let alone a parent.

Instead of trying to drain love from a spouse or children, go to real friends for help, those with strong, healthy real selves. This could be a parent substitute or a good therapist. You can even go to God, and eventually to your own real self. If you are still single and find your love bucket empty, learn to fill yourself up *before* you marry. You will be ready for the giving that is the core of marriage and parenthood and the heart of all forms of real love. Spouses and children are giving places; God, self and others are taking places.

Fear of Criticism

Shyness and boastfulness are two common behavioral patterns that are associated with children of poor parenting. Children of poorly grounded parents may develop certain common, predictable cover-ups to hide the pain they feel at being used to fill their parents' empty love buckets. Especially common is the reaction of a child whose parents get their feeling of worth from the child's performances. A child in this type of family environment will expect to do everything right because that is what his parents hope for. Obviously, a young child is unable to live up to those high standards of performance. That child will develop a great fear of criticism. This type of child may develop a shy cover-up, which is underacting, or the opposite—a boastful cover-up—that is an overacting.

Parents who don't know their beautiful real selves often think their worth is determined by the things they do, and of course, by the things their children do. If you believe this, wouldn't you want to win when you play cards or become one of the top salesmen in your field? Wouldn't you also want your child to be a great athlete, or an outstanding student getting "A's," or even becoming student body president? You would because, in your mind, performance would determine personal worth. A mistake on your part or a failed test on your son's or daughter's part may be alarming? Yes.

These kind of parents are perfectionists and usually give too much criticism in the home. They exaggerate the importance of orderliness and performance and so they also use their children's performance to measure their own internal worth. They firmly adhere to the old adage, "Behind every good child is a good father or mother." It is a little different twist on the saying, "Behind every good man is a good woman." (His mother of course.)

Perfectionists and "clean freaks" are terrified of the "mess" inside of them—the feeling of chaos and failure. They have so much pain, anger, helplessness, and confusion internally from raped feelings of childhood. They *must*, at all costs, cover this up and compensate for it, by external orderliness and success. It's easier to control externals than this internal, painful mess. They are driven by this intensely.

If these parents have a child who doesn't read by age four or five, or doesn't make first string on the varsity team, or whatever is important to the parents, then that parent feels personally threatened. Success and failure mean too much. Mistakes are viewed as failures.

Mistakes are not failures. *They are learning devices.* Now that is quite different. Think about the way a baby learns to speak. How many times will she babble sounds that no one recognizes? Hundreds, thousands of times. Do we call those mistakes? No. We know that she is trying out sounds and learning, through trial and error, which ones will make words and get responses. We don't criticize her for learning this way. Neither should we criticize older children who are still learning. Actually, our entire life is a learning experience. We all learn by trial and error. We have the right to fail.

When we are critical of children for learning through the process of trial and error, we brainwash them into thinking that they are inadequate. Instead of feelings of "I'm good for nothing," we need to cause those children to feel right and productive. Let them know that it is all right to make mistakes, that it is part of learning. Next time improvement may come. This method reassures the child and encourages a belief in his or her adequacy. Perfection is: heading in the right direction.

A boy from a home where trial-and-error type learning is unacceptable will develop a fear of criticism. This will come because he has received so much of it. He'll think that every time he says or does something another person doesn't like or agrees with, he will be criticized—a well established pattern he has learned from past experiences.

So in his pain layer is a lurking, scary feeling of inadequacy. His negative self tells him he is stupid or clumsy or boring or lazy. Now this boy needs a cover-up to survive under such treatment. What can he do? As with other types of cover-ups, he has two choices. He can choose an unders style and become withdrawn and shy, or he can select an overs style and become a show off, workaholic, etc.

A person with a shy cover-up avoids the risk of being humiliated by withdrawing. If he doesn't speak up, then no one can criticize him. If he doesn't try out for the play, he won't be turned down. "Better safe than sorry," he says.

He will seldom speak out in a group, especially a new group. Nevertheless, after he gets to know the people in the group, he will talk, as long as others don't criticize him. If someone does find fault, he will do a cover-up. It is usual for this type of child, raised as he has been, to slam shut the door and, like a turtle, go inside his shell. He will become a pleaser, trying to figure out what others want him to do and say. In this way he avoids being criticized. He is surviving in a loveless world. But he feels it is worth it. At least he is safe. He is forced to worship safety instead of his real self.

By contrast, the child with an overs style may use bragging to cover-up his pain. He exhibits lots of false confidence, talking loudly about all his marvelous accomplishments and discoveries. His motto is, "I can do anything better than you." Since he expects to hear criticism whenever another person opens his mouth, the boaster tries to beat everyone else to the punch or drown others out if they have already begun to talk.

The child will seem conceited and full of superiority feelings, but in reality he has the same fears and feelings of inadequacy as the shy person. Both are afraid to make mistakes. They just have different styles of the same negative cover-up.

Sometimes these braggarts are people who were very shy until they gained fame by excelling at something—the star football quarterback or the captain of the top-ranked school debate team. Now they have changed their negative styles from unders to overs, but these new negative styles still cover the same inadequacy feelings. Though this appears as a 180-degree switch, sick is still sick.

Both the shy person and the boaster need to recognize that if we can identify our mistakes, we can learn and grow. They need to know that making a mistake does not cause everything else to go wrong. People are not all-or-none, meaning all good or all bad. Not all people are like our parents. We have blind spots and clear spots. When we make a mistake that is obvious to others, or when others can see our negative cover-ups for what they really are, we need to say, "I'm glad you can see my negative self. Help me get rid of it." Keep in mind that you can't fight an enemy you can't see.

When we can do this, we are well on the way to trusting our real selves to handle the jobs of life and getting rid of the negative cover-ups that keep our real selves from shining brightly. Winning over the false self and using it for a learning device is the very thing that strengthens our real self and gets us an "A" in the Earth School.

Task Orientation

We have already said that some parents tend to be critical and perfectionistic when they overemphasize performance. Many parents fall into this next category as overly task-oriented people. To them performance equals worth. Task-oriented persons use work—getting things done—as a love substitute and a cover-up. They are often afraid of others to some degree. They may be afraid of emotional closeness that often consists of gut-level feelings, so they escape this fear and get a substitute feeling of worth by working very single mindedly.

Most of these people choose an overs style; we call them workaholics or perfectionists. Others like the unders version of task orientation. They are the avoiders of work, often called shirkers or lazy, or procrastinators.

The overs who are the task-oriented group measure their worth by the quantity or quality of work they get done. Workaholics strive for quantity, asking themselves how much work they can accomplish. While the perfectionists strive for quality and state that "*this must be done right at all costs.*" Workaholics work too much, too long, too hard. They are very intense people. If they are not actually at work, they let their minds dwell on work, even while others around them are relaxing.

The perfectionist cannot accept mistakes as normal learning devices. This person is preoccupied *with doing it right*. They often wind up doing it wrong. As a result, neither kind of task-oriented person has time to do the things that really count, like playing games such as "horsey" with their preschool-age children, or tossing a ball with their school-age child, sledding with their third grader, or back packing with a teenager. These parents are too busy working to do much loving or learning. And that is a case of messed-up priorities. This dad will be the richest man in the grave yard!

If these task-oriented people would take the time to listen to their real selves, they would realize that real happiness does not come from professional success. Real happiness has little to do with external conditional values, which is why we are unable to fix internal problems by changing external conditions. Trying to do that is like trying to cure cancer with a band-aid. It won't work. We need to get to the deep-down causes. (Discussed in chapter five.) We can't go on merely patching the hurt—patch, patch, patch. Don't treat symptoms without causes.

In contrast to the overs task-oriented person is the unders type. These are the avoiders. She is as mixed up as the overs. She never quite gets around to doing the job at hand, even though she thinks about it constantly.

Often, these types of unders moan and groan about having so much to do. This person often curses self for not getting started sooner. But she can usually find a task which will put off the really important one. She will say, "I have to clean off my desk before I can tackle this report." Since this person also believes that work is the measure of worth, she is always the loser. She never feels adequate as a person due to her never-caught-up-with-her-work attitude. Work is always staring her in the face.

These people—and it could be any of us—are sometimes called lazy by other false selves. As we finish sentences, "I am lazy because . . ." ten times, we often find out that it boils down to rebellion against perceived authority (making them do this or that work) or rebellion against the whole insult to their identity, that performance equals worth. This is usually passive rebellion in unders styles, and active rebellion in overs styles of our false self.

Laziness can also come from fear of failure and ridicule, so procrastination may occur. As we finish these sentences for ourselves, if we are lazy or procrastinate jobs, we will see one or the other, or mixtures of both (rebellion and fear of failure).

Both unders and overs task-oriented people learned while they were children that work is the measure of personal worth. Someone gave them conditional love—which really isn't love—on the basis of how much or how well they performed a job. But it is impossible to determine internal worth by how well a person does a job. By the same token, internal worth cannot be judged or rated by external performance. That is backwards. External performance flows from internal motivation. In a healthy person, the work flows outward naturally, as an expression of the beautiful self inside. And if the person's work is temporarily stopped by something beyond the worker's control, he doesn't feel that his adequacy and worth are threatened. The person who is aware of his true inner identity is not driven by his performance. He is not nervous or worried about his work. He has little pressure. He does his best and learns from his mistakes. His performance is driven by his innate worth. His love of life gives *meaning* to any performance, not the other way around. And so the saying, "Healthy people play at life and the others work at it."

You Can't Fight an Unseen Enemy

The negative cover-ups discussed in this chapter are only five ways people try to hide their pain layer. There are a few thousand other ways. This pain comes from feeling inadequate or unlovable, whether by an overs or an unders style. At this point, you may wonder why we need all this detailed explanation of how a negative self works. It is because you can't fight an enemy you can't see, remember?

We all have some kind of negative-self layer. Since we all have imperfect parents, in this Earth School of Hard Knocks, we came to learn and grow by overcoming our problems, since none of us has received ideal treatment all the time. If you think you have, life hasn't got your attention yet! So in order to get rid of the negative layer of clouds and let the real self shine through, we need to know and understand the origin and function of our own negative selves, and that they are learning devices for the refinement of our real selves.

If I can get to know my negative-self styles well enough, pretty soon I'll be able to see them coming over me. At this point I can say to those around me, "Oh, no. I can feel my negative self coming out. I'm getting mad. I'm going to my room. Now, why do I feel angry?" Then after a few minutes of catharsis, I might be able to perceive something like this, "When you beat me at golf, my negative self told me I was incapable and inadequate. . . . Now what does my real self have to say about that? Does my worth have anything to do with winning or losing a game of golf?" The answer should be obvious by now.

The whole (cognitive) point is that we can help conquer our negative selves by understanding how they work and how they were learned, what gets us going and what styles work best. When we know and let others know this about our negative styles, then we can see the enemy clearly, and we can fight it and win. Then all of us are allies in the war against false selves.

When this in itself doesn't work, a deeper, more affective or emotional feeling-type work must be done. "You cannot *heal* what you cannot *feel*," is a great truth. Re-experience childhood pain, fear, anger. Let all the stored-up feelings come out, safely, with another loving person in their real self or privately. This person could be your own or another adult's real self, loving your inner child of the past. There is much more on this when we get to love supplies from yourself.

Chapter Four
Bodies or Beings

All of us have bodies, and inside our body dwells an inner being that entered at birth. It is the part of us that thinks, feels, decides, questions, and directs the body's movements positively. It is that self that people retain after they die. We cannot always see this inner being—the real self—with our eyes but we can feel it in our hearts and study it in our minds. Most of our lives, all we see is the external package—which is the body or the house in which the real self lives.

The body is so tangible and changeable, yet the hidden real self is fixed and always present. So many of us are confused as to the true function of the body in relationship to the real self. Often we equate our bodies with ourselves. This is where we fail to understand the body and the spirit self. Some of us use our bodies to try and prove our goodness or worth. If we know more about our real self, we will not have to try and prove anything physically. We will know and feel how lovable, capable, and precious we truly are, and that our body is a learning device.

When our bodies have not been properly held and hugged and stroked as children, we may seek too intensely for physical gratification as adults. And when we do, the body becomes far too important in our life's goals.

People who use their bodies to get a false feeling of joy often pick physical love substitutes: sex, drugs (cigarettes, and alcohol), or excess food. In the process they become sick or over weight. They may also buy clothing, diet to an extreme, body build be violent, and a dozen other ways of gratifying the physical self. But most of this does nothing for the real self. One plastic surgeon said that he has patients who are "cosmetic surgery junkies." Most of those seeking to refine the outer self do more than focus on the physical. They rely on the exterior self. They do drugs that help them to feel good, calm nerves, or excite. There are a host of other aids in the quest for physical gratification. Certainly, these people are grossly misled in their pursuit of the physical. The ladder they are ascending is leaning against the *wrong* wall.

All these things can easily be used as negative cover-ups for the pain of feeling unloved. One of the major physically-related cover-ups is sex abuse. The misuse of the body's special power to tenderly express sincere romantic love and to create children, is debased and prostituted. Clearly, some people seek far too much physical gratification here, making the physical very disproportional in importance. Sex is a *minor* part of a healthy, romantic relationship, not a major part.

Healthy Sexuality vs. Sex Abuse

Let's talk about healthy sexuality versus sex abuse before we discuss the other ways of using the body to cover up for a feeling of being of little worth or just plain no good.

Before we discuss sexuality in any special form, it is important to know that there are three different definitions of the purpose of sexual contact. *Definition number one* says it is impossible to separate sexual contact from its procreative power. A necessary prerequisite for any kind of sexual contact is an unselfish willingness and keen desire to provide a permanent, secure, loving home and family for any child born as a result of sexual union.

Under this definition sex is special, precious, private and sacred. It ought to be treated reverently. Its central purpose is to create life, though not its sole purpose. Many have lost sight of this fact. This definition requires that sex exist in a permanent, legal, and responsible, love relationship.

Any sex outside of this kind of permanent relationship constitutes *sex abuse*. That includes casual heterosexual affairs and temporary "live-in" relationships as well as all homosexuality, bestiality, incest, and child sexual abuse.

The latter four are all a prostitution of the purpose of sex because there can be no procreation and rarely is there lasting love. But the casual heterosexual affairs may be an even worse form of abuse due to the common place acceptance of this relationship as "normal."

Think what will happen to the children of people who go from one sexual relationship to another. Will they grow up with any concept of a stable home and family life? most likely not. They appear to have no immediate role models in stable, lasting relationships. What is worse, they will learn to sexualize missing love supplies as their "parents" do.

Definition number two says that any sexual contact between two consenting adults is okay. Sexual contact, they insist is good and necessary for healthy people. This definition ignores the importance of deep and lasting love, commitment and responsibility. It purports that sex can be used for recreation, entertainment, or to fill all kinds of unmet emotional needs, such as (1) proving one's adequacy as a female or male, (2) increasing emotional closeness when people fail to talk intimately, (3) strengthening a relationship, or (4) to sexualize a missing parents love in their childhood.

Some who define sex in this way feel there is no abuse of sex unless there is force such as rape or child abuse. Among both homosexuals and heterosexuals who accept definition number two there is a much greater incidence of infidelity, sexually transmitted diseases, abortions, rape, and incest than among those who accept definition one.

The *third* and last *definition* of sex which many subscribe to these days, is that before marriage you should use definition number two, and after marriage you should use definition number one. Put this way, it really sounds laughable since it is so difficult to deeply switch from number two to number one psychologically and emotionally. A promiscuous past is hard to trust in a new, sexually exclusive relationship.

Healthy Sexual Relationships

A good sexual relationship is much like a relationship in which two people weep together for joy. In order to be able to "let go" enough to cry with someone you must trust them; you must depend on them in the right way; you must have some permanency with them. In other words you need to know them over a long period of time or extremely well. This requires responsibility and concern for the other person. This is where closeness and respect come into play. In this kind of relationship, a deep, emotional union is required which honors deep felt feelings with no shame in any way. These all have to be in place. When all this properly combines, a healthy sexual relationship can result.

What would you think of someone who says, "We should go to a weeping workshop and learn to cry together better. Or he might say, "There is a brand new book on weeping." You would laugh, wouldn't you? Why would you need to *learn* how to cry? Every human being already knows how. It would be silly to emphasize the actual physical performance of crying by saying, "You cried twenty-seven tears in three minutes, and I only cried ten. That is unfair." It would be equally silly to say, "How come you get satisfaction when you cry and I don't?" Healthy people do not keep score when it comes to crying. What if someone while looking at his watch said, "The national average for weeping is three times a week. Marie, we haven't wept together for four days. Isn't it time we had some weeping? No one cries on schedule. You don't do that unless your feeling center was raped as a child and rigid performance took over.

Well, sex is a lot like weeping together. It is one optional way to express an emotional and verbal union between two people, as crying together is one optional way to express empathy, concern and love. People in healthy relationships use lots of other ways besides sex (and besides weeping) to express their emotional union. They enter into deep talking, listening, simple hugging, hand holding, doing helpful things for each other without being asked. It may be any thing that they enjoy doing together that is wholesome and rewarding to each other.

Sex is overvalued and overused as the one and only way to express this union. Indeed sex is not the ultimate form of closeness. Some of our closest, most permanent ties are non-sexual, as with our children, our parents, our siblings, and our God.

True sexual closeness is always preceded by (1) emotional feelings of closeness, where a man and a woman have a deep felt attraction spirit to spirit. They enjoy *a mystic bond*, not merely body chemistry. This bond leads to (2) a verbal union or long and deep talks about each other's feelings or *mutual self disclosure*. Healthy lovers talk about their feelings, not just their external performances.Then this verbal closeness can develop into (3) non-sexual physical closeness or affection. Healthy people touch non-sexually a lot. Sick people rarely do. They let sex take its place or they are cold and physically distant.

These three steps: emotional, verbal and non-sexual physical unions must precede the next, (4) sexual closeness. This step four is *only one* optional way of many to celebrate steps one through three in a marriage, or a permanent romantic union.

Children born in this kind of a relationship have a much higher possibility of self actualization and happiness. Since this is one optional way to celebrate the former steps, it can never be forced, coerced, expected or anyone's *duty*. It must flow, be spontaneous, natural, two-way, or it isn't a fruit of real love. It is rape.

Indeed, the false self says, "we can create steps three, two, and one by doing sex. Such sexualization or *reversing* of these essential steps of love will poison and block the growth of our real selves and ruin our romance. It was the famous Eric From who said, "Sex without true love will estrange two people."

In a healthy love relationship partners do not need one another to *prove* to themselves that they are lovable capable, good people. They do not base relationships on sex or to fill mutual emptiness by these love substitutes. Instead, the two lovers *share from their fullness* in a romance, where one real self is attracted in a healthy way to the other. They share a sexual relationship for the right reasons, to express and celebrate their inner selves and their bonding. Their interactions are very considerate, unselfish and giving. Neither one needs the other to make himself happy. They make themselves happy, as these lines from a poem by Thoreau describe:

When my life is complete without you, my friend, I will call you.
You will come to a palace,
Not an almshouse (poor house)

In a family, one love reservoir which every member of the family draws from is filled by the healthy love relationship of the father and mother. If they have this healthy relationship, and that includes a healthy sexual relationship, then the children receive the love they need in order to grow and become well-adjusted adults and parents, to fill their children's love reservoir in turn. If they don't, all is not lost. You

Real love needs to be fed, yet it feeds itself best by its own fruits. The Bible teaches that "love begets love." What does that mean? If you love somebody, you want their highest development and happiness. You sacrifice for them. You also desire to please their real self in every way. In short, you crave the best for them. Giving in this way causes them to love you even more—real self to real self.

Some of the fruits of love are hugs, embraces of appreciation, a compliment that points out the admired character traits of the partner, such as her kindness, and her power. These fruits of love feed love quite like a tree reproduces and feeds itself by its own leaves and seeds. Out of the fruits of the tree come the seeds which make new trees, as is discussed in the next chapter where I write of real love supplies.

Nowhere in this description of a healthy love relationship is sex listed as a necessary ingredient. It can be another fruit of love, in the kind of permanent unit where children are welcome. But it isn't the only fruit of love. Indeed, sex is a minor part of a healthy romantic union.

Emotional, verbal, physical unions precede sex

* Neg. Self	Real Self	
(1) ↑	(1) ↓	Feeling Closeness, emotional union, or mystic bonding - precedes -
(2) ↑	(2) ↓	Verbal closeness, long talks, deep talks, verbal union - precedes -
(3) ↑	(3) ↓	Non-sexual physical closeness or affection (N.S.P.A.) (see #3 in Love Supplies Chart, page 75) - precedes -
(4) N.S.	(4) R.S.	Sexual Union, sexual closeness as one *optional* way between a man and a woman to celebrate steps 1-3 (above) in a permanent romantic union.

* Notice the false or negative self goes backwards. It says sexual union #4 will create union #3, 2, 1 physical, verbal, emotional! Just the oposite is true. "Sex without true love estranges two people."

— *Eric Fromm*

Figure 6

Misuse of Sex

Since sex is unitive, procreative, and an expression of something innate (the mystic bond) that flows from our beautiful and capable inner selves, then using it to prove or get anything is a prostitution of the real identity and purpose of sex. Yet, people misuse sex all the time by using it to prove themselves or their adequacy as men or women, to patch up fights, or to substitute for private, personal talks and emotional closeness. Or, the most common is to sexualize missing love supplies from childhood.

In reality, however, sex is helpless to prove anything, not femaleness or maleness. It does not prove love or anything else. Sex is an expression of something you already *are*. It is an outward performance which flows from an internal bonding, it is one specialized channel of romantic self-expression.

When sex is used for wrong reasons, problems such as frigidity, impotence, force, affairs, disease, jealousy, and violent arguments arise. Frigidity and impotence are the results of an unders style. Often they are reactions to partners's using sexual performance to prove their love and worth, demanding too much of each other. The unders person would rather turn off psychologically, emotionally and physically than have his or her sexual performance used to shore up the other's false self and likely be evaluated and criticized.

The person who seeks too much sex, especially sexual affairs outside of the marriage relationship has an overs style. He or she may be aggressively grasping for proof of adequacy or love and is trying too hard, or wanting too much. The very word "sexualize" means to use sex as a love substitute. When our parents did not love us correctly, we sought to sexualize that missing parent's love. We can heterosexualize a missing parent or homosexualize a missing parent.

Often men in therapy finish the sentence "I need sex with other women because . . . ten times, as fast as they can speak. The answers nearly always reveal a missing mother's genuine and exclusive physical bonding early in childhood.

Bi-sexual and homosexual patients honestly finishing the appropriate sentences reveal the same loss and need now to sexualize that love with the same sex parent in a fake "romance." Such sex is to fill the illusion of permanency, possession, and exclusiveness missed in the early parent child relationship. How superficial for a homosexual patient or his therapist to think he's "cured" when he can now heterosexualize his missing love supplies instead of homosexualize them or vice versa! The problem to "cure" is the sexualization (sex abuse), not the choice of a partner. This is only a symptom, not the cause.

All false selves are formed when we have to survive as children in an abusive home. Abuse is any non-identity treatment, usually shame. It comes in many ways: emotionally, verbally, physically, and sexually. Whenever we are used as though we were someone else's property, this is abuse.

Sexual abuse can be done emotionally, verbally,and physically. People sexually abused in childhood are deeply affected for life, especially without psychotherapy. They will overdo or underdo sex. Overdoing sex is repeating childhood. Identifying with our sex abuser to deliver us from the helpless trapped feeling of our childhood victimization is one cause of overdoing sex.

Identifying with parents' false selves and learning their styles gave us survival *power* and a way out of helplessness and shame. A man who goes from one woman to the next is often punishing the mother of his childhood and at the same time trying to find a good mother in every sexual conquest.

Many men still have breast fixations because in infancy stage (0-9 months) they were not nursed correctly or at all. Others have anal and buttocks fixations coming from poor love supplies in toddler stage (9 month to 3 years) when potty training was not naturally allowed. Genital obsessions can come from weird treatment in this and the preschool stage (3-5 years) when parents do not understand sex in its true identity. Lusts of all kinds may go back to childhood and so, one lasting way to solve these is *re-experiencing childhood feelings* in these stages with a loving, safe person—giving the little child of the past *the love he never got.* Shaming people with sex problems is a continuation of the very thing that causes these sex problems.

Homosexuality is also a type of sexual misuse among people who subscribe to definition number two. They feel that their sexual contact is not bad or immoral and that they should be free from any discrimination by others. While we may disagree with this moral point of view, it's important to remember that because a person may have a block or a hang-up in one area does not mean that that person is "sick" in all other areas of his life.

Some theorists insist that all people are bisexual early in life, that everyone initially wants physical affection or sexual contact with both males and females. However, as a person grows older she or he usually begins to seek physical affection from the opposite sex only. This constitutes a maturing of sexual identity, they say.

When homosexual people seek psychotherapy to change their sexual *preference*, very often the therapist notices that the history of the problem is (1) some sort of difficulty with the opposite sex, and (2) a lack of love from the same-sex parent. This part is like a phobia that traces back to the parent of the opposite sex, who has placed too many emotional demands on the child.

For instance, if a woman is living her life completely for her children—getting all her purpose and meaning from them, she may be over-indulgent with her children, spoiling them, and needing them to like her.

If a mother is seductive, that is, if she knowingly or unknowingly uses subtle seductive non-verbal cues in her interactions with her children, the male child will often feel very inadequate. This is due to the fact that he can't fulfill her needs, either emotionally or sexually. He may then feel guilty and uncomfortable around females and may want to stay away from any contact in which a woman could demand that he perform in some way—like his mother did. This obviously includes sexual contact. Combine this with a lack of physical affection, caring, attention, and identification with the same sex parent, and the young boy or man is likely to seek that affection from males who are his peers or older. The affection will later on be sexualized for illusions of identification, permanency, possession and exclusivity.

When a father actually dislikes or detests his son, that son cannot make a male gender identification. He does not want to be male, and if so, then there is a problem. Studies show that between eighteen months to two years is the ideal time for a male to identify with his father. If this does not happen then, it becomes increasingly more difficult as time goes on.

In many cases, a male child will identify more with the mother, especially if she needs him to. He could be effeminate and/or seek the lost father else where. All homosexual males are not effeminate, however.

Also, the notion that homosexuality is biologically caused or genetically caused is just as ridiculous as heterosexuality being organically caused, especially if heterosexual activity is solely for the purpose of love substitutes and not reproduction. Homosexual relationships are more turbulent and fickle than heterosexual ones.

I once had a homosexual patient who was terrified that researchers might find a biological cause for his homosexuality and be able to correct it biologically. He was afraid that he would have to stop his actions and could never again have sex with his same sex lover. I assured him that it was truly a *preference* and he need not fear.

The concept of "gay" is a socio-political movement in our society. It has nothing to with the real problem of homosexualizing a missing parent. There are increasing numbers of "non-gay" homosexuals. This problem can be and has been "cured" by effective psychotherapy when the patient sincerely desires the change and works with a therapist who believes it can happen. This is a prerequisite for all change through therapy. No one would go to a therapist to change something he didn't want to change, nor would he go to a therapist who didn't believe it could be "fixed."

The above could apply in reverse to a daughter with a very demanding, needy father who is in some way seductive and a mother who dislikes her early in life. Not every person in such a situation becomes a homosexual, however. If there are five or six children in a family where parents have many unmet emotional needs and are also seductive, perhaps one or two will have homosexual tendencies. There are several other ways a child can choose to deal with over-indulgent or needy parents who may also be seductive, and most of the children will likely chose other lifestyles we have mentioned.

Homosexuality is just one kind of misuse of the body, as are heterosexual problems such as rape, or child abuse. There are many other ways in which the body can be used to gain a substitute feeling of worth that have little to do with sex. These are the body hang-ups that may seem perfectly harmless to most people. But if they are motivated by a deficiency of real love, they are not harmless at all. They prostitute the body. They perpetuate the negative self and strengthen the cover-up later. Sexualizing our missing mother or father is usually the core cause of sexual addiction, whether in heterosexuality or homosexuality. The abuse of self is a greater problem than the specifics of the sex addiction.

Other Physically Related Love Substitutes
1. Appearance

A socially acceptable and even socially encouraged negative cover-up for people who are convinced that their bodies are the "real me" is to concentrate too much of their attention on their appearance. Often they think every hair must be in place each time they step out of doors, or that the latest style clothing is an absolute necessity.

They may diet fanatically so as to be super-slim, or any number of other fad items to appear thin, beautiful, and alluring. The point is they want people to look at their bodies, not their real selves. They don't trust or know their real selves, so they use their bodies as a substitute to try and get some feelings of worth.

Often a person with an appearance cover-up dresses in such a way that you can't see his or her real self, even though you know it must be there. If a woman is being seductive, she will present her body as the most obvious thing for you to relate to, and that is her problem. If you get too busy looking at her body to notice her real self, then that's your problem. Look into people's eyes to see the inner beauty, and *then* notice their beautiful bodies, which are only secondary at best. When we get old and wrinkled and gray, appearances can't continue to be that important or matter. But real self, and love, can be stronger than ever then; that's when healthy people often grow to love each other even more deeply than ever before.

2. Oral Gratification

Oral gratification is a cover-up in which people use their mouths as love substitutes. They eat, drink or smoke or chew too much and at inappropriate times. Instead of letting their real selves handle problems, fears or worries, they give the job to their mouths.

I once knew a boy named Tim who was a good example of this. The kids at school called him Tiny Tim, yet he weighed three hundred pounds. One day I asked Tim what he did when he was up tight. He then told me, "When that happens, I smoke cigarettes, chew gum, eat Mound bars (he had three bars in his pocket while we conversed), and drink Cokes or coffee. And if I'm scared, I bite my fingernails." Tiny Tim wasn't giving the job of handling anxiety to his real self; he was giving it to his mouth.

A person develops this kind of negative cover-up as a result of experiences when very young. Someone whose mother was anxious and fearful of his crying, and coped with it by sticking a bottle or a pacifier in his mouth, probably learned that his mouth should do the jobs of his real self. As he grew older, he learned to bite his nails or suck his thumb, to feel warm, calm and safe.

Later, Tim discovered the magic of food, which not only satisfied his oral infant needs, but stimulated his taste buds and provided a feeling of fullness as well. Everyone knows about the full feeling resulting from overeating. Why do so many people seek this feeling of fullness? It has to do with the identity emptiness inside.

Those who don't get enough oral gratification from food often use cigarettes, which not only elicit the sucking reflex, but provide a chemical "high" or rush and create a feeling of fullness in the lungs. Many overweight people typically say, "When I smoke, I don't gain weight. I get the full feeling without calories." What a modern miracle! A person can get a full feeling on bran, and without calories, and no rush either, and no cancer or heart disease.

Besides providing this feeling of fullness, cigarettes calm the nervous system and create a sort of sedative. But smoking is life-shortening and stupid, though it works for some in the present. Like all drugs, after they calm you down, they tighten you back up as well. Like all negative cover-ups and love substitutes, they give you a momentary *illusion* that you are filled, important and desirable, but they leave you even more empty at the end. It's simple. The people who use their mouth for gratification get something for nothing and nothing for something. You can never get enough of what you *don't* need.

In therapy we see many overweight people, women especially, who want to get rid of their extra weight. First we try to discover what their emotional pay-offs are and where they first learned about these pay-offs for over-eating. Over the years, we have discovered some of the most common ones to be these:

1) *Being overweight is an escape from being female.* The overweight patient often discovers that she does not like being female because of all the negative things it means to her. She thinks femininity means staying home most of the time raising kids, cleaning toilets, serving and being a sex object. This is a negative view, but it probably summarizes her perspective when she was twelve to thirteen, entering puberty.

At that point she was threatened by the physical changes which signaled her unavoidable womanhood. She was also threatened by the complex social relationships looming ahead.

Also, she didn't like the way the boys responded to her. She worried if she didn't have a date and also if she did. All this was too much for her to cope with, so she decided to eat her way into escape through a fat body. This, of course, is a prostituted body, but it became a welcome defense for her. All she had to say to herself when no one asked her out on a date was, "Well, it's because I'm fat," (rejection protection). In this way she avoided all the scary and unpleasant aspects of being female. Surveys show that most grossly overweight women have been sexually abused in childhood. You can also starve yourself (as in anorexia) to reduce femaleness.

2) *Being overweight proves others love me for my real self.* This is confused thinking. One young lady said, "My mother constantly told me, 'No one wants a fat girl like you.' So, then I decided I would prove to her that she was wrong, wrong, wrong. I would get fat as a pig and still get married. Then she

would see that a man could love the real me, even in a fat body," (revenge and rebellion).

This woman wasn't only trying to prove it to herself, but to her mom as well. Her negative self convinced her that her mother was right all those years. She decided her overweight body made her "no good." Now she is using her fat body as her negative cover-up, using it to prove her lovableness. The real self doesn't do that. It doesn't have to prove anything and it doesn't prostitute bodies, they are too sacred. Her negative self is in charge, and only a negative man will hook up with her, fat or thin. She also loves to rebel against mom. It gives her an illusion of freedom, when she's really a slave to food and to rebellion.

3)   *Food equals love; it's a substitute for closeness.* Overweight patients often say that all their memories of warm, happy times with family members or friends revolve around food. Desserts or meals or drinks seem to be the magic things which bring closeness and love. One young girl said, "The only time my dad was really nice to me was when I baked bread or pies or a cake for him. I had a good feeling when we sat down to eat my baking together." These kinds of people begin to equate food with love and warmth and then to seek good feelings by eating, not to mention the sweet taste experience in their mouths when they eat.

4)   *Food gives me a "full" feeling.* When people feel emotionally empty, whether they realize they do or not, they look for things to fill themselves up. And, though it's not logical, food can seem to be the perfect thing. The mouth is stimulated or "turned on" and the stomach feels filled up. But a sweet experience in the mouth is not the same thing as a sweet experience in the heart. Here again, food is acting as a substitute for love. It is the mirage of an oasis in the desert. But the body is not you. You can't fix internal emptiness by an external body fullness or sweetness.

One patient who had never been overweight said she gained fifteen pounds while she was in therapy learning to uncover her negative layers and dig into her "garbage pile."

Then when she discovered her real self and saw what a lovable and capable person she really was, she lost the extra weight effortlessly in a few weeks. She quit feeling empty and therefore didn't need to keep filling herself up with food.

These examples of overweight cover-ups are just a few of many, and they really constitute an over-simplification of a very complex individual problem. However, the pay-offs listed for overeating offer some guidelines for beginning to understand this complex problem. Finish this sentence ten times as fast as you can go. "I'm overweight because . . . ." See what payoffs come up for you. These are reasons or rewards that keep hang-ups going.

3. Drugs

Both legal and illegal drugs are used by people in our society who want to cover up or run away from their pain. There is aspirin, caffeine, nicotine and alcohol, as well as marijuana, cocaine, amphetamines, crack, depressants, and the list goes on. These are supposed to offer people turn-ons or turn-offs. They provide escapes in the form of extra energy, euphoria, stupor, or altered consciousness states, all of which are love substitutes, cover-ups for pain of negative feelings.

Alcohol is one of the most popular drugs in our society. It offers two types of negative cover-ups at once—a drug and an oral gratification. It calms, dulls pain, and relaxes while filling the mouth and stomach with a tingle and a good taste. Now that's a winning combination. Coffee is much the same thing. It stimulates the central nervous system and "rushes" the heart. So in that sense, it's a very potent drug, an upper. It also gives the mouth something to do and fills the stomach with warmth.

Again, the big lie is that the body needs to turn on. Those who know and trust their real selves feel loved and competent, able to cope with the world. They don't need drugs to help them feel better, because they already feel so good. In fact, they don't want anything interfering with their ability to feel, taste, touch, smell, hear, or see. They love themselves and they know that the best, highest, and deepest feelings come through the real self, not its substitutes. The cure to all these is love supplies, not a band aid over a cancer.

4. Psychosomatic Illness

Psychosomatic illness is illness caused by a person's mental or emotional condition (consciously or unconsciously). For instance, migraine headaches and ulcers are usually psychosomatic, resulting from worry or fear or anger turned inward. Some family doctors have said that seventy-five percent of the ailments they treat are not physically caused, but are emotional in origin.

These kinds of illnesses can be connected to feelings of inadequacy or incompetence. They can be used to achieve lots of different goals: to provide an escape from the things one fears, such as, "If I get sick, I won't have to present my report in front of everyone today." or to gain attention, "People will notice my absence and come to see me if I'm sick; they'll bring flowers if I'm really sick." and of course to play the martyr, "I work so hard but no one even appreciates me. I'll get sick and then see if they miss me and all I do for them." Then there are those who confirm a negative self-concept, "I'm no good to anybody. I can't accomplish a thing because I am always sick with something or other," and there are many more.

The first step in treating a person with psychosomatic illness is to find out what it is he fears. Once you know that, you can help the person face the fear and deal with it. Then comes the recognition that the real self is extremely capable of solving problems. What a pity and a detour or even a decoy when a fearful person says a psychogenic illness is caused by the body only.

When a person selects a negative cover-up, she often picks one that handles two or three needs at once. For example, a woman who "chooses" psychosomatic illness as a negative cover-up may need attention from others due to a feeling that others don't appreciate her special talents. People scarcely notice whether she is present or not. But she may also be afraid to interact with others, fearing that they will see her mistakes and criticize her. So she uses constant illnesses to try to meet both needs. Extra attention can be gained through sickness, and if she doesn't have to extend herself, work with others, or compete to get it, she doesn't have to risk anything, especially failure.

If the person is to get rid of this illness, she will have to deal with both needs. The real self might learn to handle one job, that of expressing talents, being a little more outgoing and letting others see her uniqueness more, but if she doesn't deal with the fear, she will still need her psychosomatic illness to cover it up. Until she learns healthy ways to fill all the needs attached to this one negative cover up, it won't disappear. This kind of change is sometimes very difficult and requires consistent effort.

Any person who wants to give up negative cover-ups and let his real self emerge to handle more of the jobs of life must want to change with his whole heart. Otherwise he will not be willing to pay the price for that change such as re-experiencing childhood pain and anger with a real loving person.

Harmony Between Insides and Outsides

It is becoming increasingly popular and tempting to theorize that our problems are all biologically or organically caused. One theory will discover abnormal anatomy, another a gene peculiarity, or another a chemical imbalance. They all allege that this is the cause of our problem. Often sick people will jump on the band wagon because these "discoveries" give them the out or escape from guilt or blame they are trying to hide from or ignore.

To my knowledge, there are no valid, correctly done studies which *prove* these theories to date. Even if there were, none of these findings can prove if these chemical imbalances are causes or effects. In other words, depressed people, by their constant pain and anger, held deep inside, could well cause chemical imbalances in their neuro-transmitters, which can be corrected by valid psychotherapy far better than chemicals alone, which put a band aid over their emotional cancers. It is true, there are some people who cannot benefit from psychotherapy and must have these pills always, but they are a minority. Millions of dollars are made annually by the well meaning pill pushers. Way too many people use them to mask their feelings and stop them from the therapy that would *cure* the cause.

The physical body is often misused by people who are trying to fill their empty love buckets to cover-up their pain layers. The body is a marvelous tool for learning, yet we often forget that it is such a tool. The body is not the real self, however it is often mistaken for the real self. Remember that the body is a vital shell, but the real self is inside.

The body is a temple, meaning a physical dwelling place for a holy, spiritual presence. Our bodies are indeed temples, the dwelling places for our beautiful inner beings or our spirit selves. Without the self, there is no uniqueness, no identity, and no life for the physical body. It is totally dependent on the inner self.

When we experience real love for our inner child of the past, we get in touch with our real selves, strip away the layers of false cover-ups, and safely feel painful negative feelings. Then we can use our bodies in a natural way to express the feelings of our beautiful inner selves, instead of exploiting bodies by making them servants of our negative selves. When the real self is in charge of the body, there is matching harmony that is inside and outside. Actions and words fit perfectly with non-verbal cues and inner feelings. We say that such a person is congruent or authentic. In other words, he is real. And how does he get that way? The answer to that question is the subject of the remainder of this book.

In our relationships with others we must be in contact with our real selves or we will misuse others and never find the true joy of living. There are many things we can do to perfect our understanding and make more contact with our real self. The following chapters offer ways we can accomplish this.

Part Two
CONQUER YOUR ENEMY

Chapter Five
Real Love Supplies

When a human being is supported, loved, and honored as a precious, worthwhile person without doing anything, this is primary love.

When he or she is wanted, loved, understood, taught, spent time with, and played with, this is true love.

Did your parents enjoy being with you, take an interest in your interests? Did your parents love you when you made mistakes? Did they help you without asking, stay with you when hurting or angry or afraid? Did they confirm that you were OK by showing this in a thousand different ways? Did they honor your feelings and needs joyfully? If yes, then you had primary love, identity love, internal love, or unconditional love.

Of course, it could never have done what love does unless you received it and it came along as part of a way of life.

This kind of real-self love is called *primary love*. It is the foundation type of love, in which the love target is internal, it is your real person. Ideally, children should receive all the primary love they need from their parents. This comes from family love reservoirs. If they do, then ideally their real selves will grow strong and be able to handle the jobs of life and grow from them.

Individuals who receive lots of wholesome primary love as children are also the most likely to succeed at romance, which is a different kind of love, a higher type. In a healthy romance, the two people give to each other from mostly full love buckets. It takes two strong real selves to make this well-founded romance work.

The main difference between romantic love and primary love relationships is the person. Primary love relationships help nurture someone whose life needs filling. If it is a child, his identity bucket is being filled. Romantic love is two full people sharing.

Favorite Love Supplies

How can those who haven't had enough of the real thing when they were young get filled up with love? It is the same with adults who have grown up physically, but whose real selves are barely known to them. Both must accomplish two things that will help supply this love: 1) They must find an excellent *source* of real love; that is, someone with a strong, healthy real self who knows the difference between primary love and romance and also between giving and taking. 2) They must learn to let the love come into them. Each of us can learn to benefit from love by being a good sender and a good receiver of love supplies.

The second part, *receiving love,* is hard for many people, especially if they are older and have large cover-ups that they have been shielding for years. A lady named Jane is a good example. Her real self is very faint. It is hidden by large doses of pain and a lot of cover-ups. She received very little unconditional love as a child.

One of Jane's favorite cover-ups is overconcern with her appearance. Her hair, her make-up, her clothes, all must be perfect. If not, she feels incomplete. Certainly she does the right thing by grooming properly and caring for her physical body, but Jane has gone overboard on the whole issue—its importance in her life. When I have advised her that her eyes sparkle and I can see the real person inside, she may think to herself that it is the new mascara she is using.

You see, Jane is so conditioned to think her worth comes from externals, she has a difficult time absorbing the real love she is offered. Instead, her negative self perverts it, grabs it and twists it. Why? She is using it to feed her cover-ups instead of letting her real self have a chance to receive it and say that she is inwardly beautiful. When she does reach the point of allowing her real self to come shining through, she will feel, "I'm real. My beautiful real self exists."

Even though Jane has had lots of people giving her compliments and advice, until she learns to make some new channels for the real love to flow in, like the channel that directs the path of a river, her real self will not receive that love. She needs to become aware that her negative self grabs away love supplies. This leaves a void. She hasn't received them. She must let her real self have that love, but she can't. Awareness alone is not enough.

There are many ways to receive love, probably as many different ways as there are people to give love. We all have our favorite love supplies. These are the best ones for us and the deepest, most direct channels for receiving real love which nourishes our real self.

Here are six things that someone else can do for us to bring us back into our real self when our negatives are trying to take charge. Here is a list of some basic favorite love supplies of those I have talked about:

1. *Listening and understanding.* Close, private talking in which the listener refrains from talking too much, rather, the listener feels and has *empathy* as a listener. This is seeing things through the other person's eyes.

2. *Reassurance, praise, and encouragement*. Telling the person how you love and respect and treasure his real self. This helps him to believe in it again. This can be called *verbal affection*.

3. *Hugging or holding*. This is not sexual. It is primary love, the kind little babies need so much of. Lots of good, real love can flow from one person to another through physical closeness if the one giving the hugs is truly giving and not taking anything. This is often referred to as *physical affection*.

4. *Privacy and trust*. Quiet time alone, away from everyone else, to let the real self come back out and try again, or trusting someone to learn alone from their mistakes.

5. *Explanations*, teaching, telling, feedback, advice, counsel, direction, guidance. Best only when asked for.

6. *Firmness*. Setting limits or boundaries without holding back on love. This includes loving the person while stopping or disapproving negative actions. It is protecting a person when they cannot protect themselves. This avoids harm. (See the Love Supplies chart on page 75)

The first three are *tenderness* forms of love. The latter three are *power* forms. All of these are excellent love supplies. We'll talk about each of them in detail as we discuss empathy, openness, and firmness. Not all six love supplies work equally well for everyone. Most people have one or two favorites that will nearly always help them get back into their real selves, ones they have missed a lot.

Now if you know what your favorite love supplies are, you can tell your friends and family members what to do to help you when your negative self is in charge. You might even tell them what signals to watch for so they'll know when your negative is starting to take over. Describe your negative self to your family and close friends. They can help you fight it much more effectively if they're able to recognize it right away. Of course, if they are this wonderful, your false self will be small.

We did this sometimes in our family. Once I was telling my children how to recognize my negative self. I said it was loud and overbearing, that it sometimes yelled, and that it did put-downs. My son, David, piped up with another addition to my list when he said,

"Dad, when you are in your negative, you have a sarcastic, hostile laugh."

"I do?"

"Yes, you do." He then pointed out that the laugh belittled others and made him feel shamed and stupid.

I appreciated his observation later on. It helped me to improve. Pretty soon everyone knew how to tell when Dad really needed a big dose of his favorite love supply.

This kind of approach makes sense when you consider how we treat other types of illnesses. It is a fact that having your negative self take control of you is like being physically sick. If you have some kind of serious illness that could strike any time, you'd want your family and friends to know what to do should you have some sort of attack or onset, wouldn't you? You would say something like, "When you see me start to go like this and begin shaking, run to my purse and pull out the little white pill bottle.. Put two of them in my mouth and force me to swallow."

You'd make certain that they know all about your medication or whatever is required to assist you. This saves lives in many homes.

The same thing is true while dealing with negative self "attacks." Often in just a few minutes, with the right help, you can be yourself again. Later, you'll learn how past wounds (like phobias) can help predict when the negative self will "strike." In order for others to assist, they need to know the symptoms and remedy. The old adage is true in this case: "A spoonful of sugar (love) helps the medicine go down."

The Basics of Love: Empathy, Openness, and Firmness

Real, primary love is essential for encouraging the inner self to grow. So what is it? What is it made of, how is it expressed, and how do I know I'm receiving it? Love is a deep mystic feeling. These are its expressions at best.

True unconditional love has some necessary ingredients. They are as follows:

1. *Empathy*. This comes from deep respect for human feeling; it is the ability to listen, understand, and be sensitive, to feel the feeling of others, and communicate back to them.

2. *Openness*. This is the ability to openly express true feelings, bringing them out in the open verbally, emotionally, and physically. It stems from admiration and reverence for human feeling

3. *Firmness*. This is an ability to discipline or teach, to observe a single standard of conduct and obedience to the laws of reality, and to take the consequences of all one's own actions.

If you look at the list of favorite love supplies, you'll see that the first is an example of empathy; the second, third and fifth are openness; and the sixth is firmness. The fourth one, privacy and trust, will be discussed in the following chapter also as love supplies from self.

These three ingredients of real love—empathy, openness, and firmness—always nourish both parts of the real self: the soft, tender, lovable part and the powerful, protecting, capable part. Empathy and openness nourish the lovable part of the real self with kindness, gentleness, understanding, and hugs; and the trust and explanations and firmness feed the capable part with instruction, realistic expectations, and consequences.

If these two parts of the real self are fed together, then the person will grow to possess a beautiful blend of tenderness and power. Unfortunately, however, most of us have difficulty giving or receiving *all* the ingredients or expressions of love. Often as parents we give too much firmness without enough empathy and openness. We are simply too strict. If we give too much empathy with little firmness, we become too permissive. Are we referees or cheerleaders?

One great psychologist claimed that the successful counselor must have both firmness and warmth. Teddy Roosevelt hit close to the mark when he said, "Speak softly and carry a big stick." In a scriptural context, one reads much the same thing: "Reproving betimes with sharpness, then showing forth afterwards an increase of love." This is real, complete love.

Empathy or Honoring Feelings

Empathy is an avenue through the external cover-ups and the pain layer to the real self. Not surprisingly, it is the first thing on the list of favorite love supplies. Some people are afraid of empathy. They don't want to deal with their own deep feelings, especially not the negative feelings in the pain layer. They would rather stay on the surface and see only the cover-ups. But those who do use empathy will eventually get through the pain layer to the beautiful, glowing, real self inside; then they will experience deep emotional unions, the kind that others will never know. You cannot heal what you cannot feel. And you can't feel until it's safe to feel.

Empathy is listening and understanding, neither agreeing nor disagreeing. It doesn't include giving advice. To empathize, you must follow the person's lead and discover how he or she feels. It is recognizing that the other person knows the solution to his problem somewhere in his heart. He knows more about himself than you will ever know. Empathy demonstrates faith in the other. It can be summed up in the statement, "No one cares how much you know until he knows how much you care."

Lots of people confuse empathy with advice. They wonder why their children get angry when they suggest a solution to a problem the youngster has confided to them. They need to realize that people in the midst of strong emotions can't listen to constructive criticism, or even possible solutions at that moment, no matter how true and logical they may be or how carefully worded. It is bad timing.

What a person in this position needs is *emotional first aid.* Someone to understand first and simply accept what is going on inside him; someone to give empathy. Then, after he feels loved, accepted, and understood, he will have more strength to deal with the problems. At that point he can be given advice, if it is really necessary. You can do the cleaning and dressing of the wound and even major surgery later if necessary, but the first thing to do is to give first aid in the form of listening and acceptance of feelings underneath the words.

In order to give the best kind of empathy, the kind that will help others the most, it's important to understand something about how people think. There are three basic ways or modes of mental processing: visual (seeing), auditory (hearing), and kinesthetic (feeling).

People who use primarily visual channels see mental pictures; they are affected most by the sight of things. They like a tidy room, a trimmed lawn, an exotic painting. They usually speak in terms of seeing. They will say, "I don't *see* why you act this way," or "It *looks* to me like . . .," or "I *see* what you mean."

Auditory processing depends on hearing. People who like to use this mode pay a lot of attention to sounds. They often talk to themselves, carrying on inner conversations in which they ask themselves questions and tell themselves answers. They may remember events in terms of the sounds associated with them: the crashing waves at a beach party or the silent stillness of a cross-country skiing expedition. Sometimes it's hard for them to listen to others because they are hearing their *own internal voice* at the same time you're talking to them. These people will say, "I *hear* what you are saying," or "That doesn't *sound* right to me."

The third processing mode is kinesthetic, based on feelings. People who use this one a lot check their feelings to find out what they think. They want to know, "How does this *feel*?" They may combine visual and kinesthetic modes by seeing a mental picture first, then checking their feelings to find out whether the image is a pleasant or an unpleasant one. Keep in mind that all this occurs within fractions of a second. We seldom realize what we are doing. These people often say such things as, "I could *feel* everything that the speaker described," or "This just doesn't *feel* right to me."

Each person you meet will usually have one or two dominant modes of thinking. For instance, one person might be mostly visual and kinesthetic, another mostly auditory and kinesthetic, and a third may be primarily auditory. Most people use all three modes, but to varying degrees. They have favorites. Not many people are exclusively attached to one. It helps to know what a person's dominant modes of mental processing are, but those aren't necessarily his only modes.

Now, how can this information be used to give good accurate empathy? One way is to learn to speak each other's language; in other words, to get ourselves into the same mode that the other person is in. If we can notice what kinds of statements the other person is making and whether he's using *see*, *hear*, or *feel* words, we can help him to feel understood by using those same kinds of statements ourselves. Here are the 4 Cs of giving empathy:

1. Capture the feeling under the words
2. Compare this feeling with your past feeling experience
3. Communicate back to them the feeling captured and compared.
4. Carefully respect the talking and listening turns

Step One: Capture the feeling under the words

Feelings are the engine to the train. Performances are the caboose. Most people have this backwards; they think performance equals worth. The truth is, earth birth equals worth. Feelings are your very essence. What good is a human being who cannot feel? At very best, he is a robot who is programmed to perform. Being means feeling. Some people are human doings, not human beings.

The new baby is a feeling organism and is run ninety percent by feelings. When hurt, the baby cries; angry, he screams. Babies want respect and understanding for these feelings. When they don't get that, their feelings are shamed and they begin pleasing or rebelling to survive. Their identity is prostituted and a false self, a mutant human emerges. The little real self stops growing and is in a "feeling prison." Later on, he will have to be rescued, recovered or reclaimed by the adult real self, or else real change may not occur in the mutant self.

"Rescued" means loved. And love means honoring these aborted, shamed feelings of the past and present.

Think about how systematically our feelings are shamed in childhood. When we cry, what do adults say to us? "Don't be a sissy, or a bawl baby. Stop that whining. Go to your room. Stop crying or I'll give you something to cry about." And so the threats go on. It amounts to shaming the most precious parts of us, our feelings. This is what has been done to many adults. They were shamed in childhood and now repeat this shaming method by shaming others.

If feeling our pain was shamed, think how difficult it was for us to feel our anger! Almost impossible, and now our anger may be stuffed and frozen inside of us, covering up our true identity and making us weird. (Some have called the false self "my weird self.")

Most of these feelings must be known and recovered before we can really honor anyone's feelings. True empathy is the way feelings are honored, whether it's with ourselves or others.

To empathize we first have to really *hear* and *feel* and *see* the message of the other person. Where is he coming from? What mode of thinking does he prefer? How does he view the world? What's in his heart? What does he listen to? How does he feel? And most of all, what is his missing love supply? This doesn't mean just surface, but all the way down inside.

We can listen with our eyes, our ears, and our feelings. We hear what the words say; we see what the body language and facial expressions say. We feel what the feelings say. Words are not the most important part of a message, but words can tell us which mode or modes the person prefers. Listen especially to his verbs. Look for the action words.

Does he say, "This place *looks* a mess," or "I *feel* like having a drink," or "Let's *hear* what she has to say." Think of this as, "Let's *see* what she has to say."

Several studies of the way people send messages showed that fifty-five per cent of a message is conveyed through body posture and facial expressions, and thirty-eight per cent is conveyed through voice tone, such as pitch, volume, and rate. This leaves only seven per cent of the message to be carried by the words. So there is much more to good listening than hearing words. For example, if a person is becoming upset or anxious, the voice pitch might go up, the volume might increase, or the words might come faster.

If you notice these things as well as the words being used, you'll understand better how the person is feeling. If you are really listening, you will show it by putting down the newspaper, turning off the TV, and leaning slightly forward in the chair. And even more important, you will look the person right in the eyes. The eyes are the windows of the soul.

One girl who was especially sensitive to the many aspects of listening once referred to the *doors* of my eyes. She started to tell me something, but I was thinking about something entirely different. She spoke about two sentences, then stopped and said, "Dr. Ellsworth, the doors in your eyes just closed."

"What?"

"The doors in your eyes just closed," she repeated.

"How can you see the doors in my eyes?"

"I can. You were thinking about something else."

"You're right. I was thinking about my farm."

Now I might have said, "What do you mean, the 'doors' in my eyes just closed?" Every doctor knows there are no 'doors' in the eyeball. But she knew that I was not really with her. I was not entirely emotionally present. She knew. I was thinking about my farm. Scientifically, these "doors" are implied by things like pupil size, focusing, lateral and horizontal eye positioning. But this sensitive young woman didn't need to know anything about eye anatomy or eye movements to realize that I'd just closed off the doors of my understanding to her, and that she didn't want to be alone then; she wanted me to understand.

People are like great castles with deep moats around them and big drawbridges. They can choose to let down the drawbridge if they want others to come in. But they don't have to. No one can enter into the heart of another if *they* want to close them out. In order to understand another person's heart, to see how he really feels, you need to really listen to the message. Hear it, see it, feel it, especially in your own heart first. How can anyone deeply understand another if they can't do empathy with themselves and *feel* their own feelings?

Step Two: Comparing this feeling with your past feeling experience

As you think you are truly hearing what the other person is saying, look into your own feeling bank or reservoir to see if you have ever felt like he seems to be feeling. Sometimes you may not know how it feels to be in the exact same situation, but you will recognize *similar* feelings or emotions. For example, if you were interviewing a man in the penitentiary, and he were telling you how it feels to murder, you might look into your heart. Then you might say, "I don't know how it feels to murder." Look again, very deeply, and you will find that you don't need to know that exact feeling in order to understand him. If you have been *angry* enough to kill, that will do.

If you see intense anger or intense fear within yourself, then you are at least able to empathize. That is a start. There are those who can't see or feel intense anger.

When you sense your own anger or fear, this will better help you understand the other person's anger or fear which preceded the murder.

When a child says, "The teacher punished me."

We should not ask for more details or say, "And what did you do to deserve it?"

We need to show instead that we understand his pain and embarrassment and feelings of revenge. How do we know what he feels? We look at him, we listen to him, and we draw on our own emotional experience. What we know the child must feel when he is shamed because we have been shamed, too, and we are open to our own past feelings. As we are open to *our* feelings, we are open to the *child's* feelings.

The thing that makes step two difficult is that many people are *feeling bankrupt*. They look into their feeling reservoirs and find nothing. Sometimes the listening person can't remember when he or she did something wrong or had problems. He thinks he is too good, now. That's a feeling of bankruptcy. He has closed off from his awareness some of his own painful feelings. People who repress their unpleasant feelings cannot empathize. How could they enter into someone else's feeling world when they look inside themselves and find nothing there or nothing but denial?

You need to be a feeling person *before* you can empathize with other people's feelings. If you're all closed up, if you haven't cried for seventeen years, if you haven't been emotional for months, if you have ulcers or colitis because you are uptight, or migraines because you can't get to your real feelings, you can't be very empathetic. If your own inner child is in a feeling prison and you are in your parent's false self, you will be afraid of feeling and can't empathize. Yes, you can't heal what you can't feel.

As we mentioned earlier, a common mistake when trying to give empathy is to jump right in with a solution to the problem. What does this imply? It indicates that we think the other person is inadequate to solve his own problem. Suggesting solutions may look like empathy; it may look like someone really cares, and that's probably true, but it's *not* empathy.

It is never the listener's job to solve the problem, even though it might seem that is the goal. It is the individual's job. When the listener tries to find a solution, she has a good thing in the wrong place. It's just like planting two or three beets in the corn row of your garden. In the corn row, they are weeds. A good thing in the wrong place isn't so good any more.

So, if the situation calls for empathy, give empathy, period. Then, after the person feels your love and understanding, and only then, he might be able to receive some advice if he asks verbally or nonverbally for a solution or an explanation.

Step Three: Communicate back to them the feeling captured and compared.

When you do respond, remember that you are still on a listening turn. It isn't your turn to begin talking, except to paraphrase what the other person has relayed to you to make sure that you understand and to show that you do. He will give you a signal when he needs you to do this. This paraphrasing is a way of reflecting the message back. Then the other person will feel your empathy. The following two examples will help clarify this point.

Nine-year-old David came home from school on a very rainy day with tears running down his face. His mother could clearly see that he was upset or angry. She knew David had been planning for today's class picnic for three weeks, and now it was pouring rain. His mother could have said, "What are you crying for? or "Don't worry, there will be other picnics," or "It's not my fault. I didn't make it rain."

Instead, she put herself in David's place and listened to his lament. She watched his nonverbal message that included facial expressions of disappointment and body posture of dejection. She *felt* what he was feeling. After taking the time to understand what was bothering him, she said, "You must really be disappointed. You planned for this picnic all along and now it's raining."

After several minutes had passed, he stopped crying. A few seconds later he said, "Oh, well, there will be other days." He felt understood. And so he could cope with the situation himself. He felt loved, and love conquers many things in life.

In another instance, Julie's cousin had been visiting her all summer, and the two girls had really enjoyed one another. When it came time for the cousin to leave, Julie came running down the stairs crying. Her mother said, "Oh, don't cry. It's not such a big thing. She'll be back next summer."

How many times have we all said something to this effect? Well, Julie gave mother a hateful look for that kind of response. She felt that her mother didn't love her. She ran to her room and cried all the more.

David's mother gave empathy, understanding, kindness, and love. When she did, the problem seemed to evaporate. That's what often happens with accurate empathy. On the other hand, Julie's mother didn't empathize or try to understand. She thought only of herself. The way she reacted, there is little wonder Julie felt hateful and unloved at that moment.

Besides simply reflecting the feeling, you can help the other person feel greatly understood if you will slip into his or her mode of thinking and speak the same language. For instance, if a husband and wife are having a disagreement about clothes strewn around a bedroom, what should each one do? Mark's dominant mode is kinesthetic; Carolyn's is visual. She complained about the mess. She is bothered by the way the room looks. If he wants to be empathetic, he'll switch to the visual mode and say, "I see that you want the bedroom to look nice. The sight of this mess really gets to you." And she'll say, "Right, right, right."

Now, what if Mark is not empathizing with Carolyn, but merely arguing that the bedroom feels just fine as far as he is concerned? If she wants to give him an empathetic point of view or feeling, she can present a similar situation to him, only placing the problem into kinesthetic terms. She might say, "Looking at these clothes lying here makes me feel upset and uncomfortable. I feel like I'm lying in a bed with cracker crumbs."

This analogy is bound to give any kinesthetic person a feeling for the situation. Now perhaps Mark can sense and feel how uncomfortable the sight really is. This makes Mark *feel*. Why? Well, it's easy to see. The scene has been equated within his own realm of experience.

Step Four: Carefully respect the talking and listening terms

Accurate empathy always takes turns. If someone begins talking to you, you should use the first empathy step, which is *capturing the feeling*. Keep it in force until you get a signal to change turns. What is the signal? One lady said, "Well, I know how to tell. When Harry takes a breath, I jump in and start talking."

That is *not* the signal. The signal can be many things. Listen to voice tone when it goes down. Then watch the eyes and face looking as if they want you to respond. This is a method that demands feeling. "Do you see how I feel?" Then there is, "Well, what do you think?"

Changes in voice tone, questions, inquiring facial expressions will show you that it's your turn to talk and that the other person wants to listen. Now suppose you believe it's your turn, but when you start to talk the person doesn't even hear you. He just continues to talk. Then you know it was a false alarm. He wasn't ready to change turns yet. Go back to the first step, gather more information, look into his eyes, try to understand how he feels. You can even say, "I stole your turn."

Secure people understand that everyone can't talk at once. Someone must listen. If you study their conversation, you will see clearly distinguishable turns. Only love deprived people interrupt. Some parents interrupt often, then spank their children for interrupting!

They steal their children's speaking turns, then wonder why the children are so selfish. They wonder why the children won't listen. For people who are not considerate of turns, in conversation, it is sometimes helpful to stop and clarify whose turn it is, saying, "Who's supposed to be talking and who's supposed to be listening?" Talking turns say ninety per cent of the words and the listening turn says about ten per cent only.

When you love yourself and others, you understand how others feel. You give empathy at the right time, and you do it naturally. This flows from you because you care. You don't mind spending a lot of time in conversation using empathy to clarify things. You want to help the other person progress from the area of obvious feelings to deeper feelings, even if it is about negative feelings. Doing empathy to negative feelings will lead to true identity feelings in time.

Now let's talk about openness. Healthy people are open people. They are open verbally, physically, and emotionally.

Verbal Openness

Your real self recognizes that words are servants. They wait on the mind and offer great treats and wonderful insights into the mind and heart of the inner self. Like a good servant, your words should be faithful and reliable— true to the thoughts and intents of the heart. They should be honest, firm, and clear. A verbally open person can express feelings freely. He can and does express love. It is never a forced expression but flows naturally. He generally expresses himself in short sentences, without the overuse of words, so that others easily understand what he is saying. "The language of truth is simple and unadorned," St. Duperey said.

Openness can be expressed in three ways. 1) verbally—sharing real feelings in words, 2) physically—by hugging, and appropriate touching and 3) emotionally—by expressing feelings through laughter, crying, whistling, and singing.

The verbally open person can also express his opinion without needing others to agree with him. If you disagree, he recognizes that as your right, knowing that he is not in charge of your belief system. He is not trying to sell what he has to say. He realizes that whether you accept or reject his opinion, it has nothing to do with his own personal worth.

When you are giving love supplies to another person, your words can be sensitive to privacy at the same time they are honest and firm. Instead of saying to yourself, "I don't want to hurt your feelings, so I'll tell you lies." How about this, "I don't want to hurt your feelings, so I'll be quiet."

The verbally open person doesn't want to see others squirm or be hurt in any way. He may say, "Well, I won't be able to tell you that. It's private." Such a person is sensitive to others' feelings and recognizes that some emotions should not be shared.

Busy parents can help their children develop verbal openness by giving them a set chance to talk about their deep feelings. They might spend a few minutes of empathic listening time every day. When the children are young, an excellent listening time is just before they go to sleep. Fifteen minutes two or three times a week, while sitting on the edge of their bed, can help the children learn to share their feelings in a close, safe, home environment. But, it is far better if you can, to listen to them *when* they speak and not wait for bedtime, etc.

When children become teenagers, it is critical that they have a chance to talk to someone about their real feelings because they have so many new and strong ones. Those who don't have this chance can be like volcanoes on the verge of erupting every minute.

One such seventeen-year-old girl was referred to a newly organized school counseling clinic where she was very hesitant about talking to the counselor. However, after her first hour she told the receptionist that that was the first time she had spent a whole hour talking with an adult in her entire life. That's tragic.

When talking about their deep inner feelings, many of my patients tell me, "I could never tell this to my father. He never talks about stuff like this." Such a father, of course, is a closed-up person. He is like a husband who said to his wife, "Mary, I told you I loved you thirty years ago, and that is to stand until you hear otherwise."

There are many people who have been "word raped" in their childhood. Words may never have been used in their families to express feelings or give guidance or convey truth. Words were only used for taking love substitutes. Yelling and screaming, lying, tricking, and shaming. These were all sick head games such as "poor me," one up, guilt induction, force and threats. They were all done by the wrong use of words and they were the only use of words these people knew and know now.

In this case, words were used to *get* something and only for the moment. There was never any consistency, reality, or predictability to the use of the words. The child could not *trust* the words. That is, the words had no depth, value, or meaning beyond momentary need filling. People coming from these type III homes are often unable to benefit from or understand psychotherapy or counseling attempts to help them.

Fortunately, not many people have come from such homes where they were "word raped." Those who have, find it very difficult to receive help and have to settle for psycho-tropic medication only to help them. And that does not mean that the causes of their problems are physical only.

Physical Openness

Emotionally healthy people hug, touch, and kiss. They say, "I love you," or "I like you," or "You are a wonderful person" with physical affection. This person is not afraid of physical contact. Healthy physical openness is not used to fill a deficiency. It *gives* instead of *takes*. It's brother/sister love that we call *human family physical affection.* The hugging and holding listed among the favorite love supplies (number three) at the beginning of this chapter are this kind of physical openness.

After a woman in Eugene, Oregon heard a lecture on love supplies, she decided to prove to herself that she was a good mother by giving her fourteen-year-old son hugs. She was doing the right thing for the wrong reason. One morning after breakfast she had to chase her son around the table to catch him. Well, since fourteen is faster than forty (years-old), he ran down the sidewalk to school, and she was left standing in the doorway, crying. In her negative self, she called the school to get her son out of class to find out why he was "so mean to her." The counselor called the boy out of class and asked him, "Why are you so mean to your mother?" (which is a very defensive, stupid way to help anybody.)

The boy responded with,"Mr. Jones, do you know the difference between a hug that gives and a hug that takes?"

The counselor mused and scratched his head. "No, I guess I don't.

"That's what I thought," said the boy. "Mr Jones, when my mother hugs me, she sucks me dry. I wouldn't hug her if she were the last woman on earth."

Why does he dislike his mother's affection so much? It's not affection. She *takes* hugs; she doesn't give hugs. We cannot take love from our children to make *us feel good.* We then imply that their purpose is to nurture *us.* But it's really supposed to be the other way around. Trying to force or take love from children is feeling and hug rape.

Why can't we take love from a child? Children are not born to give us love. They are born with needs. The father and mother are required to fill their children with love. The children have identity seeds that need to be nourished. The parents' great joy and pleasure is to give, give, and give some more. It is a treat, not a treatment.

A baby's body needs holding, rocking, to be carried about, stroking, and skin contact like lying naked next to the mother whose warm, soft skin it can feel. Our skin is our largest sense organ, usually about twenty square feet in size on an average adult body.

Healthy parents can think of dozens of ways to fill the baby's need for skin contact. Nursing, of course, is an excellent example. Sleeping with mommy is another one. Baby's will wean themselves in toddler stage from sleeping with a parent just as they wean from the breast. And they will be much more able to love and be close to a loved one when they are older.

The key to fully gratifying the body in childhood is the joy and the love we feel for our baby. Duty nursing, duty holding are as stale and cold as a duty hug or kiss. A small baby has *love radar* built into its emotional being. The baby knows instantly if you don't love and treasure having that child in your life, and you cannot fool him.

As children get older, they also need to have their bodies and appearance praised verbally. Such phrases as "I love your eyes," "You have beautiful hands," and so forth are examples of this type of praise. It has to be sincere, or the child will know it is phony.

When a child's physical love needs are not filled, he will spend much of his future life looking for something that will give "body turn-ons." Food is a big one, but there are others such as sex, drugs and violence. Here are four ways guaranteed to drive a child to be a body freak, seeking only physical gratification:

1. *Body Neglect.* The body requires affection. Some parents never touch, hug, or hold the child, and some mothers refuse to nurse their babies.

2. *Body Violence.* Hitting and slapping, pulling hair, pinching, and inflicting bodily pain with sexual and physical violence.

3. *Body Taking.* When hugging and touching are done to fill up the parent's emptiness, not giving true affection to the child from the parent's fullness.

4. *Body Criticizing.* Shaming the child's body. The size, shape, color, texture of skin, bone structure, whatever.

These four ways are guaranteed to get a sexually addicted, food addicted, drug addicted, and perhaps a violent freak or bully. These ways have to be changed. Here is one example of doing this.
'   This father has a little girl he dearly loves. When he comes home, he gathers her in his arms and kisses her sincerely and asks what she has been doing. He talks to her for the next few minutes and looks in her eye, and at no one else. His attention is directed at her. He also listens to what she is telling him. He understands. She

knows he is real because there is a certain light in his eye that reveals his love. She can tell that he can't wait to be with her, and she gets the feeling that she must be very important to him, that she is a valuable person.

If we are to give physical affection as love supplies, then it is important that we really *give* and not look for anything in return. The real self has limitless amounts of love to give. There is no need to worry about running out when your real self is in charge.

Emotional Openness

Human beings are emotional beings. When their real selves are in charge, they don't try to hide their feelings. Emotionally open people can cry, sing, dance, jump, yell, laugh, or whistle without feeling silly or self-conscious. Emotionally open homes are singing, laughing, or crying places. There, people can express all their feelings openly.

A little girl in our neighborhood came over to her friend's house quite often. Once her mother said, "June, how come you are always at Catherine's?"

Her reply was, "I like to be there; it's a singing home. They sing and dance and play the guitar. They laugh and whistle and have a good time." Then she said the most cutting phrase, "Our place is like a morgue." What a statement about her own family.

Why don't children stay home? Well, what are we doing to make the home atmosphere fun and loving? Are we having any parties? Not big parties, but perhaps family parties. Are there any outings? Do we have a family evening together? Are we sharing, when the child has an opportunity to open up?

Make your family a fun family to be with. Whether you are a young parent or an old parent, or no parent at all. Be open and have family meetings, parties, and outings. It doesn't have to cost much, just do it. Make the most with what you have, but do it. The most important organization in the world is the family. But, most of all, it is the presence of real love supplies that counts and keeps children close to home, not the external activities only.

Firmness

We have seen how empathy and the three kinds of openness act as love supplies from others to the real self. This develops the lovable, tender part of our character. Empathy and openness can dispel a great deal of painful "no good" feelings and help the real self grow and shine much brighter. But if the real self doesn't also receive the third ingredient of love, firmness, it will never be fully grown.

Firmness develops the capable, powerful part of ourselves. Firmness-love is an almost absent thing in some parts of the American culture. Firmness-love implies that we love others enough to tell them the truth. We love them enough to be consistent, to be reliable, to follow through, to set limits on behavior. This also means being assertive in a gentle but resolute manner. Good firmness includes discipline, responsibility, consequences, consistency, and obedience to the laws of reality. It is done with tenderness, courtesy, privacy, and power. "There is nothing quite so gentle as real power, and nothing quite so powerful as real gentleness." (McKay)

The Single Standard

Firmness and consistency operate under a single standard. It is the same level of firmness for parents as well as for children. When consistency rules, everyone in the home obeys the laws of reality, no matter how old they are. These laws come from a higher source. They flow from Mother Nature, the universe, and God. They are not made up, so they apply to everyone. If a lie is bad for the child, it is the same for the parent. If smoking is harmful to the child, it is the same for the parent. Stealing is wrong for the parent as well as the child. There can be no double standard.

Children from homes where the single standard is applied, love and respect authority. They see authority figures as allies on their team to teach the laws of reality which they themselves obey. They do not see them as enemy agents, as in inconsistent, whimsical homes. This is due in part to parents who know right from wrong and exemplify it in the home with firmness and confidence. All of us recognize that by obeying the *laws of reality*, we can become truly free. In the same way, the astronauts, by knowing and following to the letter the physical laws of the universe, are free from the surface of the earth and can soar into space, going all the way to the moon. But certain laws must be followed to attain such results in flight. If they make one tiny error or mistake, they may destroy their craft, resulting in death or being miles off course. True freedom comes from obedience to the laws of reality.

Consistency

Consistency is the essence of firmness. It means that the consequences of an act are administered *every time*. Think about the way Mother Nature teaches a nine-month-old child to walk. She applies the consequences of falling down which usually results in a bump. This is always repeated, and soon the child learns not to fall down. Similarly, the very first time the child touches a hot stove and gets burned, there is learning that is immediate. Usually, the warning comes without being told. The child has to know that if he does a certain destructive act, the consequence will be consistently the same.

Parents, if you tell a child to do something right, be sure that he does it. Later on is the time to talk about the results. Perhaps this talking could come during evening empathy time. However, you'll have a smoother family life if the child can be sure you really mean it when you set proper limits on essential, life-threatening behaviors, not on every little thing.

Decide ahead of time which things are worth the trouble you will have to expend to enforce the rule. Children should receive immediate consequences when they overstep the limits. For example, you may say, "Freddy, when you hit Benjamin, you have to go to your room (or the current phrase, 'take time out') and we'll talk." "If you throw your food on the floor, you won't get any more for dinner." Make sure you make it stick, just the way you said it. Only say it once.

I used to have a little puppy that came with me each evening to help me milk the cow. For months that little puppy laid down by the back feet of the cow. I told that puppy every evening, "You're going to get stepped on if you stay there." But she doesn't speak English, so she would just look up at me and wag her tail. Well, about two weeks later it finally happened. The cow stepped right on the dog's foot. That changed everything. She no longer wanted to come near the cow. One time. That was all it took.

Is the cow mean? No, she didn't even know the dog was there. Does the dog think the cow is mean? No, that's silly. The dog simply has a healthy respect for the cow's movements. That is the way discipline for our actions ought to be. It is a simple act of natural consequences without anger or meanness. "Natural" consequences are never hitting, anger, whimsical, or other forms of identity abuse, and certainly *never* withdrawal of your love.

Children Need Limits

A magazine article entitled "Kids Who Steal" illustrated the need children have for consistency and firm limits. The article tells of one small town's problem with stealing among its seven-to-nine-year-old children. After examining the problem, the parents found that if they would do four specific things, the children would stop stealing:

1. They were to have regular mealtimes (with meals).
2. They were to have regular, consistent bedtimes.
3. Parents were to work out regular chores with the children.
4. Parents were always to know where the children were and were always to let them know where the parents were.

Parents who put this information to work found success. They set up regular mealtimes, bedtimes, and did a better job of keeping track of their children. But, they had one item that seemed so difficult: chores.

When they overlooked having the children responsible for work, they made a mistake. The parents were like the mother who felt that it would be easier to wash the dishes and do other little things herself. It would be less trouble and the job would get done. Some of the parents tried for a while to give their children chores, but were no good at following through. They lacked consistency.

Why should children have chores to perform? Because chores are a natural consequence of living. Almost everyone who has ever lived has had to dispose of his garbage in some manner, clean up after meals, and keep the place clean. Living causes dirt. Increasing filth is a health hazard and must be tended to. When children learn at a young age that part of the price of enjoying good food and an orderly environment is to help keep it that way, they become more responsible if it's done lovingly. They must learn that life is no free ride. They must somehow see first-hand natural consequences of their failure to help.

In a well-organized family, parents do not have to constantly remind their children of chores to be done. Instead, you might use a chore chart, listing the names of the children and their work assignments. This can function exceptionally well if you let the children have some options and help in making the work assignments, especially as they get older.

When children participate in choosing their jobs, they feel better about doing them. One night a week could be set aside for a family meeting to discuss family business. The children might decide that each one will do two chores a day, or they might want to have one person do all the chores for one day and then have five days free. One family lets its members choose their jobs each week, rotating who chooses first. The important thing is always to have something for each child to do and to make sure that he knows what is expected.

Once when I was explaining this to another father, he said to me, "Sterling, do you have any pink shirts that were white before your kids put them in the wash?" (Doing family laundry was one of five chores rotated in our family.)

"I sure do. But do you know how many white shirts I can buy for the cost of one therapy session for one of my children a few years from now?" Sometimes we don't count the high cost of not teaching our children responsibility.

One family uses a system of grading to handle chores. This isn't the ideal system, but it's one example of what you might do. We have an "A" for super job, a "C" if the child is sloppy, but does the job, and an "F" if he or she doesn't do the job at all.

Every day each child receives a grade, and at the end of the week we add up the marks. The one with the highest chore grades gets a money reward. This is for excellence. Some families do it differently. They pay an allowance based on so many dollars per "A" grade performance. For "Fs" he receives nothing. The children under this system of performance receive an allowance according to work accomplished. We also have the children do some work that they don't receive money for, which gives them the opportunity for both types of learning. You can use other consequences besides money to accomplish chores. We discovered that we could avoid nagging at our children by posting a sign near our dinner table that read, "A good meal for a clean room." Every night before supper I toured the children's rooms to see whose was tidy and whose wasn't.

If Bill's room didn't pass inspection, he didn't get to eat until it's was clean. At that point, he usually dropped his chin, stares hard at the chicken dinner on the table, and moans, "When I get back from cleaning my room, there will only be wings left." He would dash up to his room and tidy it up. This is using consequences, not anger, to get the job done. It works, especially where food is concerned. Take a lesson from Mother Nature and let the consequences do the nagging.

Regular mealtimes and bedtimes also teach children consistency. At our home during the school year we had a set bedtime, usually 9:00 P.M. The older children were not required to go to sleep at that time, but they had to go to their rooms and either read or do something relaxing. It really didn't matter, so long as they were in their rooms.

After 9:00 P.M. was my time that I enjoyed spending alone or with my wife. She is more important to me than all the others. I want to spend some time alone with her. From 6:00 A.M. to 9:00 P.M. is for the children and their needs. We have our needs too, but they come later. This sort of boundary helps children to develop respect and consideration for others.

All of these techniques work *only* when the other love supplies are present in abundance. Some people feel all this would naturally flow if there was deep love in the family.

Discipline

Discipline comes from the word *disciple*, which means a student who learns from a great teacher. So discipline must teach, and for it to have effect, it must honor the true identity of the learner and fix causes, not just symptoms.

Ashley Montagu said, "The child needs no discipline but the discipline of love." I am convinced that if a baby were greatly wanted, greatly respected, and honored by a healthy parent from birth, there would be little need for all the rules and regulations and laws that are required in today's normally neurotic society.

A child who is honored in all his feelings and respected as noble and precious will not do all the bad things most parents complain of. The bullies, the passive and active rebels, the shy, the drug and sex abusers, all retain false selves that are caused by a lack of supplies in childhood. Little children love to be loved. They want to please. They are loving by nature, and only when their true identity as curious, bright, feeling beings has been shamed and squashed do they become mean, violent, selfish, and lazy.

Most of the so-called problems parents bring up are caused by the parents, but they don't see it that way. When a child makes mistakes, parents should see through the eyes of the child. Place yourself in their situation. What is really going on with your child? You will not think of some of the things she is doing as evil, maybe just misdirected, confused, curious, or seeking love.

Once a mother told me that she sent her seven-year-old son to bed. The boy refused to go and said, "No, I don't want to go to bed!" The mom was ready to discipline her son in the wrong way. She wanted to strike him, threaten, argue, and shame him into going to bed. Then she remembered our motto which is, "Honor feelings." She put herself in his place and said, "Oh, I see. It's no fun to go back to your room all alone and be in the dark with your door shut. You would rather be out here laughing and watching TV and eating popcorn with us. Sure you would. It is more fun, isn't it?" The kid couldn't believe his ears! His mom was seeing through his eyes and hitting it exactly right. She was remembering how she felt at seven when it came to her bedtime.

The boy responded with, "Do you know that kind of stuff?" The mother replied, "Sure. I used to be seven. Let's go see what we can do to make your bedtime more fun. What do you think we can do?" The boy had three great suggestions: leave the door open; leave a small light on; and read him a story. Was that asking too much? I don't think so. Every time a child does something wrong, look for the missing love supply, and then give it to them. If you can't, go to your room to get back into your real self, then come out and give it to them.

Discipline is better when it's consistent, which means it needs to be administered when a parent is calm. What, then, should you do to discipline a child who does something wrong? Here is one recipe:

1. Restrain the child or control the act, (such as pulling the child away from another to control hitting).

2. Find the cause of the wrong doing.

3. Treat the cause.

These last two steps sometimes require a lot of effort on the parents' part. They must ask the child how he is feeling and listen with empathy to what he says. They must realize that a child who does the wrong thing for the wrong reason feels deficient, inadequate, or unloved. His negative self is temporarily in charge. They must understand what the child's payoff is for the bad behavior and try to give real love supplies to help the child's real self take control again, so the payoff isn't necessary anymore.

Sometimes a child does need to be "punished." But that doesn't mean he needs to be humiliated, or treated with disrespect, or with severity. The purpose of punishment is to help the child understand, obey, and enjoy the laws of reality, not to give parents a release for all their own hostilities. It should set an example; it should help a child learn to eventually develop his own inner controls. Appropriate consequences are especially effective for young children eight and under. If they learn to respect and obey the laws of reality at a young age, most children will need very little correcting when they are older.

Appropriate consequences for young children might include sitting on a chair for several minutes, being sent to a time-out room, or having their activities restricted.

I no longer believe in spanking in *any* form. This has gotten out of hand in our society. When a child's body is used to satisfy a parent's intense feelings, it teaches the child to abuse his own or other's bodies later on with like violence or with food, sex, and drugs (which abuse their own bodies). They will resort to these things to appease intense feelings of rejection and physical abuse.

Any parent who will get alone with a child and see through the child's eyes, honor and understand the child's deep feelings, will be able to "solve" the problems, no matter how difficult the situation, and see the problem in an entirely different way *than* using physical pain to discipline. A child would only say that he had a spanking coming to please or idealize a sick parent.

It is very important for the parent to do inner child work with his own inner child and his real self for this to work. This is explained more fully when we talk about "rescuing your inner child" yet to come. Of course, any punishment should be followed by an increased demonstration of love toward the child.

One father said, "Dr. Ellsworth, what is the time span between sharpness and an increase in love?"

"Three or four minutes. Why do you ask?"

"I can't speak to my children for days after I punish them. I'm so mad and I feel so mean."

As this father uses the silent treatment, what is he teaching his child? He is implying that the child did such a bad thing that he isn't worthy of his father's company, or even conversation. He is, for that period of time, rejecting the child by withdrawing his love. The child is probably hating himself. In contrast, the healthy parent shows an increase in love after discipline to let the child know that he is still very much loved. The child knows why the parent was firm with him. Then the parent gives him a hug and says, "I love you. You're a good person, but we all learn from our mistakes, and we all make them—even me."   This approach helps the child recognize that he is really lovable and capable, but that he must obey the laws of reality. This also separates the child's *real self* from the *action*. "You are not what you do. You are a lovable, capable, precious being, no matter what." Your identity is *not* your adversity.

The parents' firmness, with an increase of love afterwards, helps the child to do better in the future. This kind of treatment, which is consistent restraint, consequences when necessary, and loving reassurance, ultimately produces one of the most wonderful results of good firmness, and that is respect for reality.

Firmness is not meanness. It is a love supply that will help prepare children for the trials of life. Give your children true love by caring enough to be firm with them.

Sometimes firmness or assertiveness takes the form of "feedback." This is when we need to firmly say, "no" or explain something we feel a person needs to take a look at. A good method is the "feedback sandwich."

This "feedback sandwich" consists of saying a very good thing about the person. It is like cheese in the sandwich. Then say the *assertion*, like "no," or the insight (the meat), then say another praise form, more cheese and and mayonnaise in the sandwich. It might come out something like this:

"I know you want me to come to your house for dinner. How kind of you to ask me. *I won't be able to come.* I'm so sorry because I know you are a wonderful cook. Can I come another time?"

If you look closely, you can see the "layers" in the sandwich. Be sure all the layers are true. This can be greatly prostituted by false or phony people.

Another great assertiveness skill is "broken record." Here we give our firmness by repeating over and over the request we have, the idea we believe, or the insight we want someone to take under advisement. If they get us "off the track," it is because they are in a wound of ours and we are temporarily in our false self, which means we will overreact or undereact.

I remember once while in a "too performance oriented" part of my life, I was using "broken record" with a child about doing his chores. I was working too hard and too many hours, trying to be the richest man in the grave-yard (NS). I said to the child, "Honey, I want you to do your chores now." He responded, "But none of the other kids on the block have to do chores." I passed over this comeback and repeated my initial request, saying, "I know, but I want you to do your chores now." Then he dreamed up another comeback to see if he could get me off track. "You make us boys do chores, but Julie gets off scott free." I wasn't guilty of that one so I continued to play the "broken record." I said, "I hear you, but I want you to do your chores now." Soon he tried a third time to dissuade me. "You just want us to do your work for you like a bunch of slaves." I was okay with this one. I simply repeated, "I would like you to do your chores, now, honey." No empathy is used with straight assertiveness; however, it may be necessary if heavy garbage dumping, such as yelling and screaming, comes.

Finally the child hit the jackpot and got into my wound about overworking. "Of course, if you would stay home more often and play with us, we'd be happy to do chores." At this point I got mad. I broke off the record to defend my negative position. This ruined my assertiveness with myself from my own positive to my own negative self. If I had no such wound (which I later went to the bedroom to fix), I would have continued to repeat my request by saying, "I see, son. I'll try to stay home more, but I want you to do your chores now." After five or six times, being sure to look into their eyes, touch them, and call them by their first names, it usually works wonders. Especially is this true if you are "mostly in your real self." (Which I wasn't when I got off track.)

Try it sometime. I think you'll like it. It will never work in anger and frustration, I promise. You may get the external results—the chores done—but the deep causes may be worsened without real love.

Results of Real Love

The three ways of showing love we have discussed are empathy, openness, and firmness. They provide the love supplies every real self needs from others. If given in the right way, they will nourish the tiniest little real-self seed and eventually cause it to grow tall, strong, and able to carry the weight of life's big and little problems with ease, confidence, and joy.

This kind of strength comes when people have first been given accurate empathy that is attuned to their particular mode of thinking at that moment, whether in the seeing, hearing, or feeling mode. Their thoughts have been reflected in language similar to their own, and they have felt understood. They have also experienced openness in others and have learned to open up themselves verbally, physically, and emotionally. When the real self is strong, this flows easily, without fear of being wounded or rejected. And finally, they understand firmness. They have learned to

HUMAN LOVE SUPPLIES AND THEIR SUBSTITUTES

	REAL SELF		FALSE (SURVIVAL) SELF	
TENDERNESS	**Genuine Love Supplies:** (Giving)	Tally Marks	**Love Substitutes:** (same appearing or opposite) (Taking)	Tally Marks
	1. **Empathy** — listening, understanding, say back their feelings in your own words, or "un huh, I see." Put yourself in their place — see through their eyes, honor feelings.		1F. Fake empathy, agreeing or stealing turns, non-listening defensiveness: comebacks, "what ifs," and "yeah buts." Dishonor feelings, arguing.	
	2. **Verbal Affection** — Words of praise, reassurance, appreciation, encouragement, "I love you," questions to show interest and concern and any body language showing "I like you," genuine courtesy.		2F. Praise performances and appearances only, flattery or criticism, fault finding, corrections, disagree. Yelling, verbal overacting	
	3. **Physical Affection** — non-sexual touching that gives, not takes: hugs, pats, holding, rocking, cuddling, snuggling, hand holding, praise body appearance.		3F. Touch to get and take, seductive, sexual motive, or cold, distant, reserved, no physical affection. Food, sex, drugs.	
POWER	4. **Trust** — space, try it alone, "I trust you to try it again," "I trust you to learn from your mistakes." It's okay to be alone, to be on your own, to learn from your own inadequacy.		4F. Over trust, neglect, escape, or distrust, suspicion, overprotect. No space or aloneness allowed. Constant concern and surveillance. Escape.	
	5. **Explaining** — timely advice, answers, teach, instruct, solutions, questions, and finishing sentences to gain insight. (usually best only when asked for).		5F. Put-downs, sarcasm, hostile belittling, bad advice, boast, questions that complain, embarrass, humiliate. Superiority lectures, one-up, "correct-all," or no guidance, neglect, no help.	
	6. **Assertiveness** — strict, kindly discipline, setting limits, rules and consequences, with firmness and clarity.		6F. Hostile assertiveness, meanness, domineering, threatening or nonassertive, pleaser, doormat, permissive, inconsistent, ambivalent.	

Figure 7

live according to a single standard and to predict the consequences that will follow actions because of the consistency they have experienced in the past. They accept discipline.

Every person has a favorite love supply (FLS), taken from the chart on page 75. Often it is one we have not had very much of in the past. You can find out yours' and others' by asking yourself the question, "If I were mostly in my negative or false self and wanted to get out, and there were someone there I would take love from, what would I want them to do for me?"

Would it be listening, praising, hugging, space and trust, an explanation, or assertiveness? Pick the one which *you* feel will get you out of your negative self the fastest and for the longest time. Also, you may pick a backup love supply that becomes number two if number one fails.

When you know this FLS, be sure to tell it to your loved ones: spouse, parents, children, friends and others. Why? So when you are getting "weird" or stressed, and are doing overs or unders, they will know what to do for you and what love supplies to give in return. It is more powerful than any medicine you can take or give. In the long run, it can be the key to your recovery and growth.

Once in the home of a person I had just helped, I saw on the refrigerator door a love supplies chart like the one on page 75. In the tally mark spaces were the names of the children and parent whose favorite love supply it was. A little 7 or 8-year-old girl in the family was there with me, and I asked her what that chart was. She told me, "That's the world and how it works. Whenever someone in our family gets weird, we run in here to see what they need. We go out and give it to them, and they get better!"

To that little girl, it was simple. She understood that real love does make the world go round. Try it with your loved ones.

Three Ways to Raise Children

Type I. Families Full of Real Love

The highest and rarest method is to be *consumed by love*. Love is wanting and extending oneself for one's own and others' highest self-actualization. This is the desire and the action it takes for the loved one's greatest development and joy.

This type of parent is rare, perhaps five to fifteen per cent of us. The parent loves *his* life and realizes that it is his turn on earth. The parent is primarily *feeling oriented*, not just performance. He is vital and enthusiastic, with much joy to give and share. Also, there is a great positive value placed on the child. This parent greatly treasures little children, as he does his own inner child of the past. The child is a friend who is loved and treasured. The parent *likes* to be around the child, and the child knows and senses this. The parent who fits into this scope of caring and loving needs no hard, fast rules of conduct for the child—no chores, no consequences, etc. His love is so pure and strong, so constant, that the child craves to respond to this love by loving in return. Needless to say, this is a very rare home indeed!

In such a relationship, all work together, then all play together, no cops, no robbers. Look at a man and a woman deeply in love romantically. There are no rules, no signed contracts. Their feelings and words are their bond. It's simple they trust each other totally with everything. This means with the kids, with fidelity, equality, fair division of labor, goals, values, and feelings.

Since children are more pure than adults, more innocent and more perfect, we can trust them and their identity seed as we do our beloved real self spouse. "Unto such there is no law given." These Type I relationships need no discipline but the discipline of love.

Such a person will love, respect, and trust himself. He will know how valuable and precious his real self is, independent of any performance or outward appearance. And he will easily and naturally become a giver of this same kind of real love to others. Above all, he will have a zest for life, a vitality and a joy for life that will separate him from most of mankind.

Type II. Performance-oriented Families

The performance-oriented type of home is consumed with external performances. This parent greatly exaggerates success and failure as the world sees it. Performance is no longer a learning device; rather, it is a condition of personal worth. This parent weans, potty-trains, teaches to read, to do music, sports, or whatever, *for* the parent's ego needs. The child is an instrument. This fails to nourish the child's true identity seed and keeps it from blossoming. Grades at school and a host of other achievement status symbols dominate.

This family is filled with pleasers and rebels. The parent takes, not gives. The children know this deep down. The home is dysfunctional, but *pleasers* look great to the outside world. The identity seed is mutated to perform, or to rebel against performance. The educational and vocational successes of parents and children are their gods. Success is their god, and how to achieve it their religion.

These families appear wonderful to superficial onlookers. Only when the rebel side surfaces does anyone suspect what is really happening. Once again, I have to say they are doing the right things for the wrong reasons. Rules and consequences abound. Chores and allowances, groundings, punishments, rewards, charts—the whole ball of wax—are just and fair techniques for child rearing in this Type II home.

Type III. Families Concerned with Physical Gratification Only

This is the worst type of the three. This parent seeks only his own physical gratification, usually at the child's expense. Actually, these parents didn't really want children in the first place. Usually, the child come as accidents, or they want them as slaves, if they want them at all. The children know from the beginning that they are not wanted. These parents live by the flesh. They want bodily turn-ons—food, sex, drugs, violence. They hit, yell, scream, shame, threaten; all of these acts are done for their own selfish ends and gratification. Then among this type are those who neglect their children. The children run wild when the parents don't need them to satisfy some need.

This type of parent rules by emotional, verbal, physical, and sexual abuse. This is a Type III home, hands down. Needless to say, it produces very emotionally disturbed children. What is more, this type of family is common among us, especially in some economic and geographically depressed areas (though this is not always the case).

The Type I parent gives unconditional, internal, true love; Type II has extremely conditional love; and Type III has no love base at all. There can be mixtures of II and III. It would be difficult to imagine a mix of I and III.

Whatever the type of parent, many of us fall some where in the middle, and we need to explore our own real self to find the best way to convey to our children that they also have an inner self that is beautiful and capable. This is what we will explore in the coming chapters.

These three types of parents are also three types of people, the loving person, the accomplishment person, and the body person. They all attempt to initiate their style of life with whomever they associate. People unlike them are screened out and ones like them are attracted in thus the saying "Birds of a feather flock together."

So we can see that not only in parenting, but in friendships, romances, marriages, businesses, neighborhoods, churches, clubs, and whole societies, these three kinds of personalities are involved. The older these relationships get, the more one style will permeate and dominate the relationship.

Unless you are deeply aware of what kind or what you mostly are, and you really want to change, you will most likely copy the kind of home you came from. We have the free agency and will to change this. All our choices are *not* predetermined a hundred percent by how we were raised. "Where there is a will, there **is** a way." And knowing *the truth* about where we came from and the kind of home we were raised in can be one of the greatest keys to our willful change of life style.

Therefore, it is very important for all of us to choose the friends, mates, businesses, neighborhoods, churches, clubs, and so forth, that will match our style, especially if we are moving up from III to II or II to I. Happy hunting!

To summarize love supplies, I often show patients the drawing below and tell them about icebergs. Icebergs are huge mountains or small chunks of ice floating freely in the cold ocean. Whether large or small, like people, they must obey this law. About one-eighth of their mass sticks above the water's surface. This means that seven-eighths of the iceberg is *hidden* under the water's surface. The huge part under the surface is much more important and powerful than the visible part.

Every human being is like an iceberg in that you only see the surface. What you see is *not* what you get. The visible truth—often called the content, the words, the subject they talk about, the externals (appearance and performance) are only covers or symptoms of huge forces controlled underneath. Freud talked about our consciousness (awareness) and our subconsciousness (unawareness). We have talked of symptoms or acts and their causes.

There are shallow, superficial people who live by externals only. There are deep people, feeling people, who know about their causes and what lies deep inside of them and others. Our motives, our wishes and longings, our essential loving identities are under the surface and usually passed over by the masses.

There is the "external truth" and the deep-feeling truth. Laws and courts have traditionally dealt with the "facts" of an act, rarely with the deep, unseen but powerful feeling causes beneath.

When a person says or does anything, deep down they are always looking for love—the life-blood of their identity seed—or for love substitutes. They are looking to get or to share love. When we see our behavior in this way, we will understand people and icebergs much better—and we will have more joy and success in working with them, too.

When I was a little boy, my father used to quote a poem to show us the difference between the external, seen "truth," and the *deep feeling*, usually unseen. It was about a man who was killed in an automobile accident at an intersection because he had the "right-of-way;" and being absolutely "right," he refused to give way to an oncoming car. The poem went something like this:

He was right, dead right
   as he sped along,
but just as dead right
   as he was dead wrong.

Heeding the deep, unseen causes of things and the deep feelings of motives in us and in all people will prolong our lives and our happiness. "You can't judge a book by its cover," nor a person either.

When a child says she saw a dragon come out of the sky and play with her lovingly and eagerly, we don't say, "There are no such things as dragons!" We *believe* the deep feeling motives of the child. We see beyond the words; we know that the child needs love and companionship from big people (parents, teachers, and older siblings). We will immediately repent and play with that child lovingly and eagerly (and weep inside that we hadn't given her enough love).

Similarly, if a person says to his parent, "You abused me as a child" (no matter if it was emotionally, verbally, physically, or even sexually), the parent should *sense* their pain and anger underneath. Most parents stay in the surface rot and say, "I did not! How could you ever say such a horrible thing? I would never do anything like that." Or "You are splitting this family apart . . . blah, blah, blah," externalizing blame, defending themselves, suing and counter suing away all their savings. They are taking, not giving. They are continuing the very abuse they are charged with. They expose their own guilt. How much more wise and loving it would be for them to say (as in the dragon story), "That must hurt you deeply to be betrayed that way! How can I help you? I wish I could remember that abuse if it would help you, but I cannot." Of course, most abusive parents and other such people don't talk that way, or they wouldn't be abusive. But there are many such parents who have grown and learned from their past mistakes and whether they are able to remember the specific acts or not, they are willing to see through the adult child's eyes, feel *their* anger or pain, go to counseling, read books, hear tapes, or whatever it takes to help the child they now love so much. They see the whole iceberg, not just the one-eighth sticking above the water. Let us do the same.

Here is the drawing I draw for my patients. Notice the labels above and below the surface. See where "Love Supplies" is.

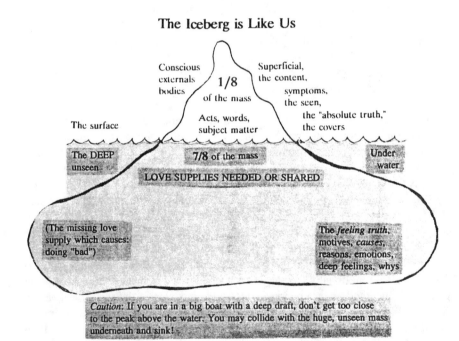

The Iceberg is Like Us

Conscious externals bodies

1/8 of the mass

Superficial, the content, symptoms, the seen, the "absolute truth," the covers

Acts, words, subject matter

The surface

The DEEP unseen

7/8 of the mass

Under water

LOVE SUPPLIES NEEDED OR SHARED

(The missing love supply which causes: doing "bad")

The *feeling truth,* motives, *causes,* reasons, emotions, deep feelings, whys

Caution: If you are in a big boat with a deep draft, don't get too close to the peak above the water. You may collide with the huge, unseen mass underneath and sink!

Figure 8

Chapter Six
Real Love Versus
Cheap Substitutes

The three basic attributes of love—empathy, openness, and firmness—all provide the good love supplies that help the real self grow and mature. The more true empathy, openness, and firmness that people receive, the more they become strong, independent, capable, secure, loving, gentle, understanding, and sincere, the closer to the core of real self they get. The real self shines brightly and our negative layers are small and thin. It's easy to see our real self, if we are searching and pondering and discovering our real self.

Distinguishing Real Love from Cheap Substitutes

Like most good or fine or precious items in life, such as gold, jewels, fragrances, these attributes of real love have their cheap substitutes or imitations. Counterfeit versions of empathy, openness, and firmness are used all the time. Many look like the real thing; others we can spot as opposites to the real thing.

And these cheap love substitutes are what cause the pain layer and negative self cover-ups to grow. We may think we are giving empathy, but often we are really doing something different. It is the negative self we are feeding, not the real self. The more cheap substitutes for love they receive, the bigger their pain layer will become. The false self grows like cancer. True empathy, for instance, is characterized by listening, no-opinion responses, understanding, and taking turns. These behaviors naturally flow for the right reasons. Those who feel empathy have a genuine love for the real self in others, and they have a sincere desire to help.

Cheap Substitutes for Empathy

Now what happens when a person trying to give empathy is motivated by wrong reasons? The following chart (figure 9) shows some cheap substitutes for empathy that result and the reasons behind them. The chart elaborates on the "right things for the right reasons" as shown in Chapter Two.

At the top of the chart are the real love supplies, which is empathy for the right reason. Then the first group of cheap substitutes for empathy are items that look like the real thing, but they are not.

They are imitations because they are done for the wrong reasons. These are the things people do when they are trying to be empathetic, but are operating from their negative selves. Questions and comments like, "Now why would you want to do that?" or "I think you are doing just fine; what's the problem?" or "Never mind, you'll feel much better in the morning." These sorts of statements illustrate the imitation empathy that is so common today. The point here is that the right thing done for the wrong reason isn't the right thing anymore. It has changed into feeling rape.

EMPATHY

BEHAVIOR EXAMPLES   MOTIVATION EXAMPLES

Real Love Supplies/Right Things   Right Reasons
   listening   love of another's real self
   no-opinion responses   desire to help
   understanding   feeling of separateness:
   taking turns   independence
   compassion

Cheap Substitutes/Wrong Things   Wrong Reasons
   (Imitations)   trying to be liked
   agreeing, reassuring   trying to be superior
   praising   needing to fix their problem
   solving other people's problems   because of discomfort with
   telling them what to do   one's own similar feelings
   questioning
   obvious "canned" paraphrasing
   exact echo repetitions

Cheap Substitutes/Wrong Things   Wrong Reasons
   (Opposites)   trying to be superior
   arguing   trying to brush off the
   come-backs   problem
   one-up-manship   discomfort with one's own
   demanding   similar problem
   threatening   (over identification)
   explaining

Figure 9

If a child says, "I am not doing very good in arithmetic," it is of little help to him to reply, "If you studied more, you would do better." That is trying to solve his problem by telling him what to do. What could such a statement imply about the child? "You're not doing well. It's all your fault. Maybe you're not a good person." This will decrease his confidence. Although he may be doing poorly in arithmetic, his statement can be met with understanding. You might reply, "Arithmetic is not always an easy subject. Sometimes the problems seem very hard to figure out." This ought to be the first step to helping the child. This is a positive reaction. If you really feel that way, it may be the best thing to say, though it is not pure empathy, it has two opinions in it. Pure empathy would be, "You're concerned about your arithmetic?"

The second group of cheap substitutes is the exact opposite of empathy. These behaviors are clearly the wrong things, but many people automatically use them when the situation really calls for empathy. These people are also motivated by the wrong reasons. They feel a need to be all-knowing, so they "explain" the child's problem to him, or they argue by saying, "No, you're not clumsy." They may feel so irritated at the mention of something which is also bothering them that they solve, threaten, and demand. They seem to want only performance and to care less about feelings.

When a child declares that he is ugly, unlucky, stupid, or bad, we cannot immediately change his self-concept by our denial or protest. That usually only brings forth a stronger declaration of his negative feelings. That is why it is the worst thing to do in a situation requiring empathy. If a child says, "I'm dumb," most of us will say, "Oh, no you're not. You are great! You're good!" And we may be right. But *at that moment* we are arguing and implying that the child is dumb because he is wrong, and wrong is dumb!

Our action fails to match our words. Once again, we're doing the wrong things for the wrong reasons. We need to draw from our feeling bank to see how he feels. We must think of a time when we felt dumb or stupid ourselves. However, we don't need to jump in and explain our experience right then. This will draw attention away from the child's feelings and concentrate it on us.

If a child says, "I am stupid," you might reply that it hurts to feel stupid, that you remember being called stupid when you were a child. The father is using empathy and a past similar experience to express concern. His understanding will help open the child for further discussion. Why? It is simple, the child *feels* safe and honest. She may say within, "He understands me . . . . He knows how I feel. I must be somebody worth understanding."

People who have not felt their stored-up or frozen feelings of pain, anger, and fear from childhood are afraid of these feelings in others. They will try to keep you and your feelings at a distance. They fear your feelings because they are terrified of their own. So these people are mostly performance oriented to escape feeling.

Emotional first aid is giving the understanding first and the advice later. After empathy, the parent can reassure the child by saying, "I think you're the greatest." Then the child may think, "If my parents understand me and consider me a fine person, perhaps I'm not worthless after all." The intimacy such communication creates may also lead the child to live up to the parent's faith in him. It is important for the parent to recognize the need for the right responses at the right time for the right reason. This takes sensitivity to others, putting ourselves in their place.

Cheap Substitutes for Openness

The following chart (figure 10) shows how verbal, physical, and emotional openness love supplies can be correctly given for the right reason or perverted into cheap substitutes by the wrong reasons.

Verbal openness is the first column on the chart, showing the real love supplies, the imitation-substitutes, and the opposite-substitutes. The motivations are in the right-hand column.

As the chart shows, people who have not seen good verbal openness in others often develop a false openness, where words are used to service unmet needs. This false openness is the imitation substitute. It may be gossiping, or showing off one's intelligence with words.

Those who seem to be open, in that they talk constantly, are often not really open at all. They may use words as a barrier or a decoy. They try to fill up all the empty spaces where one real self might touch another, always talking but never saying anything significant, especially about feelings.

Another imitation-substitute for verbal openness is subtle manipulation. Instead of saying straight out, "I want you to come to the store with me," many parents say, "Wouldn't you like to come to the store with me?" If the child answers, "No!" the real message comes out. "Well, you're going anyway, whether you want to or not, and that's that." It is much better for a parent and child if the parent makes it clear up front exactly what is expected. On some decisions, the child does not have a choice. This is firmness.

The opposite substitutes for verbal openness are the wrong things for the wrong reasons, such as lying, or being closed up, and talking briefly only about externals.

The second column lists true physical openness love supplies and their cheap substitutes. True physical openness love is a rare thing in our day. So much physical contact is motivated by wrong reasons, and people are so accustomed to the cheap substitutes that they suspect any physical openness of being the cheap substitute variety. Few people believe that a man can give human-family physical affection in the form of a hug to a woman he isn't married to, or having a sexual relationship with. For that matter, how many married men can hug and hold their wives simply to give comfort, closeness, and love without wanting sex in return? The answer? Only the healthy ones, a small per cent at best.

When we "take" our hugs and kisses, we're doing the right thing for the wrong reason. If we are hurt or angry when a son or daughter or spouse rejects our hug, we are taking, not giving. One of the great dangers of using imitation-substitutes for physical openness with children is that if you teach them to let you "take" hugs

OPENNESS
- some examples -

VERBAL OPENNESS	PHYSICAL OPENNESS	EMOTIONAL OPENNESS	MOTIVATION
Love supplies/Right things	**Love supplies/Right things**	**Love supplies/Right things**	**Love supplies/Right kind**
honest words expressing feelings silence rather than words that hurt short sentences words matching body language	hugs that give kisses that give touching to give love human-family physical affection	crying laughing singing whistling dancing	love of one's own real self, then love of other's real selves desire to share from a fullness of love and identity
Cheap substitutes/Wrong things (imitations)	**Cheap substitutes (imitations)**	**Cheap substitutes (imitations)**	**MOTIVATION** **Cheap substitutes (imitations)**
gossip questioning everything head-trips (words used to show off intelligence) subtle manipulation much talk; little said poor me swearing (using words to get attention)	hugs & kisses that take; demand seduction sex to fill unmet needs inappropriate public displays of affection lust (body used as primary object of interaction)	crying to manipulate singing to get attention showiness invasion of privacy insensitivity to timing and propriety	compensation for belief in one's unlovability and inadequacy (lies)
Cheap substitutes/Wrong things (opposites)	**Cheap substitutes (opposites)**	**Cheap substitutes (opposites)**	**MOTIVATIONS** **Cheap substitutes (opposites)**
lies little or no talk (closed up) talking only about externals (cars, jobs, politics)	fear of touching shying away awkwardness coldness, distance	no singing, laughing, or crying can't remember dreams little facial expression repression, stoicism	fear, avoidance and escape because of lies unlovable or inadequate feelings

Figure 10

and physical affection from them, then you teach them to let others do the same. Then they become easy prey later on in life, and we taught them, using the *very* thing we fear.

Many young people and adults who use seduction to try to cover up their pain and get substitute love, don't know the difference between real physical openness and its imitation-substitutes. If they have never known a hug that gave real human-family physical affection, how would they know what its substitute is? How would they tell the difference? They are doing the only thing they know how to do: they give and, in turn, are victimized by hugs that take.

Emotional openness, the third type of openness, appears in the next-to-last column. Again, the area where most of us get confused is in the imitation-substitutes. We do manipulating by crying, laughing too loud for a canned joke or situation, singing, or whistling in order to attract attention. We seek admiration and praise from others or express fake external happiness. All are motivated by love deficiency.

These things smack of hypocrisy and compensation. Most of us can sense these cheap substitutes in others, but maybe not so well in ourselves.

The opposite-substitute for emotional openness is repression. This is a lack of expression, lack of touch with one's feelings, dreams, fears, and joys. This repression is caused by fear and the desire to escape from the negative primary lies. You may think, *I am not lovable, precious, or wanted.* Or you may imagine, *I am not adequate, capable, smart, powerful.* Repression is a common way to survive when we have had a painful, shamed childhood.

Like the other two charts, this one lists the real love supplies, the imitation-substitutes, and the opposite-substitutes. In contrast to real firmness, its imitation-substitutes, also known as overreaction, are rudeness, impoliteness, selfishness, and greed. People who use these substitutes look strong because they are yelling, ranting, raving, and criticizing. Underneath they are weak, as their wrong reasons indicate. They have an *overs* temper cover-up, as discussed in Chapter Three. The bossy, over-authoritarian person is not aware of his true strength and is trying to compensate for his felt weakness. That's the wrong reason to do firmness love.

The opposite-substitutes for firmness are permissiveness and inconsistency. This often is a weak person who is constantly in a popularity contest. He wants love and fears rejection, so he usually goes against his principles to buy some love. He's the "nice guy." But he is ignorant of the beauty inside himself and of the laws of reality. This person also refuses to take the responsibility he should take with his children. Instead of saying, "I don't know what to tell you. Wait here until I find out."

"He says, you figure it out and do what you please."

This is letting the person go ahead and play jacks on the freeway. That's neglect, over trust, and permissiveness, all of which may be more poisonous to a child's character than some forms of domineering could be.

FIRMNESS

BEHAVIOR EXAMPLES

Real love supplies/Right things

clear understanding of right and
  wrong
consistent enforcement of
  consequences and limits
obedience to laws of reality
adherence to a single standard
control where necessary
strength through kindness

Cheap substitutes/Wrong things

domination
meanness, vulgarity
bossiness, over-control
manipulation, aggressiveness
humiliation, rudeness, sarcasm
hostile assertiveness
unpredictable, out-of-control
  behavior

Cheap substitutes/Wrong things
(opposites)
permissiveness, doormat-syndrome
inconsistency, weakness, shyness
adherence to double standard
pleasing, wishy-washiness
neglect
rejection by silent treatment
refusal to take responsibility
non-assertiveness

MOTIVATION EXAMPLES

Right reasons

love of one's real self and
  love of other's real selves
  (children, friends)
desire to grow and actualize
  desire to see others (children,
  friends) grow and actualize
  potential

Wrong reasons

desire for superiority and power
fear of weakness, of being controlled
desire for perfection to boost own
  ego, buy worth
desire for safety through distance
desire to hurt others, get revenge
identifying with our childhood
  abusers

Wrong reasons

fear of rejection and failure
desire for approval
lack of concern
desire for passive aggression
fatigue due to inadequacy feelings
desire to give up
ignorance of right and wrong
  (relative value system)

Figure 11

The Why Is More Important than the What

In all of our attempts to give love, whether through empathy, openness, or firmness, the motivation largely determines the outcome. If the desire to give and to honestly be what one is, comes uppermost then good love supplies will result.

If fear of emptiness or the desire to get something is uppermost, cheap substitutes will replace real-love supplies. They show in our body language, voice tone, and word choices. The problem is that usually those who give the imitation-substitutes do not realize they are motivated by a desire to get something in return, or by fear of rejection, or by re-enacting childhood pain and anger. They think they are giving real love freely. But most of us, if we will look deeply into our own hearts, are to some extent motivated by the wrong reasons. Our cover-ups for the pain of feeling shamed and our own cheap imitation-substitutes for love are so good they even have us fooled, at least on the surface.

But few of us are one hundred percent fooled. Our real selves know the difference between real love and conditional love, and if we choose to become consciously aware of our own negative self patterns and the truth about our childhood, we can. Only then can we change and grow, by accepting our feelings and learning to love ourselves as we are, without any conditions, performances, etc. Know the truth and the truth will make you free and real.

In spite of our worst negative times, can we love our positive selves as innately good and potentially great beings? If so, we will have the courage to admit our pain, anger, and fear. And we will gradually become invulnerable to the criticisms and barbs of others, safe forever from the old kind of pain. We will be unconquerable by others' negative selves. But to have this kind of *unconditional positive regard* for our real selves, we must have first experienced it from someone else, or from our own adult real self to our inner child of the past.

Many people have finally said to their therapists, "You have been the good parent I always wanted," or "You have given me the real human-family love I never had. Most of all, though, You have taught me how to love myself and introduced me to my inner child, whom I love so much."

These are the experiences people crave. They are the sole, effective ingredient in successful personal counseling or helping. This feeling of absolute unconditional love for the person's positive self makes him blossom and grow because the counselor is treating the cause of the problem. Unconditional love is only for the real self; it is not for the negative self. And yet winning over the false self is a great teacher, so we don't die dumb.

Two Self-Concepts, Two Motives

Many people seriously believe in a previous life, where we lived in an different form before coming to this planet or earth school. Still many more believe that life was very good and that our spirit selves were loved so well and so much that little children's inner self is perfect and innocent.

I like to think of us as having two self-concepts, the one in the previous life and the one we learned here on earth. I believe our pre-earth life self-concept is very positive. I raised seven children, and I never saw a child who didn't like himself, especially before the age of three or four. It was amazing to me that our infants and toddlers thought it was a real treat for us to be with them, even at 3:00 A.M. when they would wake up crying in the night.

We came to this life to be tested and tried. This is a common Judeo-Christian and Buddhist belief. Much of our testing comes from the dysfunctional homes many of us are subjected to in childhood.

There is a negative self build-up in many homes. It comes with yelling and arguing, abuse, and performance- dominated homes. The result is a negative self-concept that is brainwashed into us from earliest youth. It may take a lifetime of effort on our part to unlearn some of the lying selves we carry with us.

It will help us greatly if we think of ourselves the way we did before we came to earth, as glorious, lovable, precious people here to grow and learn from all the suffering and joy that comes to us. Keeping the pre-earth-life-self-concept instead of believing the shame and abuse of imperfect parents, friends, siblings, and teachers will make us much happier. Also, going by our previous life self-concept is much more accurate and true than going by our earth-life brainwashing from brainwashed people.

Just think what a great Type I parent we would be if we could see and believe our glorious, positive, pre-earth-life self-concept.

A Love List

We have discussed the ways people experience real love needs. Let's summarize them now by looking at a list of comments made by many people, young and old, when I asked them to list the ways in which they know they are loved. Here's what they said:

1. The person giving me love does not need or want anything back from me.

2. The loving person is firm with me. He does not please me or do whatever I ask, nor does he go against his deep feelings in order not to hurt my feelings. He is true to himself.

3. I know I am loved because she listens and understands me when I talk to her. She takes turns listening and talking and does not tell me what to do or what she thinks until I ask. I often ask. She doesn't argue. She cares what I think and feel.

4. He hugs me, holds me, or takes my hand or arm. He is not afraid of physical affection. He doesn't use this for some deficiency. It is never anything to do with sex; it's brother-sister love.

5. She trusts me, has faith and confidence in me, and gives me jobs to do. She separates my inner self from my outside performance. She knows my negative from my positive self. She loves my positive self and has patience with my "negative."

6. The loving person respects me. He makes me feel there is something precious and beautiful inside me. It's a nonverbal thing, a certain soft look in his face, admiration in his eyes, a certain tone in his voice, the way he sits or moves.

7. His love is permanent and sure because it's based on his feelings for himself. The self he loves in him is the one he loves in me. He'd have to stop loving his own inside self to stop loving mine.

8. She *wants* to be with me, yet she does not *need* to be with me. The loving person is happy when I'm near and loves to be with me, but she loves to be alone, too.

9. I know I am loved because he tells me. The person who loves me is not afraid to say it. He usually tells it like it is—good and bad. I know he'll tell me the truth because he likes the truth better than pleasing or displeasing, and he's not in charge of my feelings.

10. She knows the feeling truth of any childhood shame and has re-experienced her pain and anger honestly and openly. She continues to embrace her child of the past forever.

Cheap Substitutes List

Contrast these comments with the following descriptions of a person giving *cheap substitutes* instead of real love supplies. Which list more closely describes the love you give to others or receive from others?

1. The person giving the "love" wants and needs something back, like needing to be needed. He may be thinking, "I'll be hurt if you don't change." It's selfish, this giving to get. My behavior is used to feed his or her ego.

2. The "love" is not firm. It is weak, wishy-washy, fickle, on-again-off-again, unsettled, immature, and inconsistent. It's too pleasing, too nice, too polite; it never hurts, since the other person takes the consequences of my wrongdoing.

3. The "loving" person is always right. She argues, competes, compares. She must win. She gives lots of advice. She's demanding, bossy, threatening, too involved, or too concerned. I must please her by giving in.

4. Physical affection turns into sex. This is sex to fulfill a real-love deficiency; Sex for proof of maleness or femaleness; sex for power; dominance, or expression of hostility; sex for fake closeness to hide a real gap between us emotionally and verbally.

5. The "love" is nearly always connected with my performance or my physical appearance. It is not me he really likes; instead, it is an external condition, not my spirit self.

6. She does not really trust me. She suspects my motives, thinks I will fail. She lies to me sometimes, and I have to lie to her to get along. I must hold back my real feelings. I feel trapped.

7. He treats me as a possession. The "love" is selfish; it's usually taking. I feel used and afraid to say anything or he'll dump me.

8. The person is too dependent on me. She crashes if I go away or want to do something on my own. I feel obligated and responsible for her feelings. I am not free.

9. The person takes me for granted. Everything comes first but me. I am a sucker to stay around. Yet I'm so starved for love that it's better than nothing.

10. He has partly or totally repressed and/or denied his childhood pain, anger, and fear, and re-enacts this in his present life, especially in "love."

In comparing these two lists of some of the attributes of real love and its cheap substitutes, keep in mind that they are not all-inclusive, and conversely, that nobody will fit all the points on the list. Instead, we may see most of our own or our friend's qualities listed on the first one, the love list, and a few on the cheap substitutes list. That is what we hope for.

Remember how we said that most people are a mixture of false self and real self? Some are twenty per cent real self and eighty per cent negative self. Others are seventy percent real self and thirty percent false self, to use a simple analogy. The possibilities for different combinations are endless, but the point is that we all have some negative cover-ups and we all possess a real self.

Our future is to discover what our cover-ups are so we can gradually learn from them, shed them, and then continue to find real love supplies that will nourish and strengthen our beautiful selves so they can grow big, bright, and more beautiful. This would really be continuing and refining our positive, pre-earth life self-concept.

Being a Love Giver

Whether you are trying to help someone else or being helped yourself, the most important thing is to recognize the difference between human love supplies and their cheap substitutes. Then learn to give and receive real love. Take inventory of your own love experiences. If you haven't had enough of the right kind of love, find some valid sources and form a good dependency so your real self can grow to maturity. Then that good dependency will lead you to independence, as it must and always will. Eventually your own self and God will be able to provide most of your love supplies, and then you will be able to help nurture the real self in others.

When you can do that, you will be personally congruent. You become aware of your own authentic character traits, thoughts, and feelings. You won't try to hide your negative or unpleasant side under a false layer, neither will you wallow in it. You'll have an accepting attitude about your whole self, the good and the bad, the kind and the cruel, the achieving and the bumbling, the happy and the sad all come together to be worked out.

Healthy others will see all the parts of you, not just your public self. This is the essence of openness, though it does not mean flaunting yourself.

You will also be able to love others more unconditionally. You will see the real self in others. You will love it because it is like the real self you love inside you. You won't love the negative cover-ups people use, but you'll be able to see beneath them and know why people do what they do. You'll love the real self underneath the pain layer.

You will give empathy and openness; also you'll give firmness, nurturing both parts of the real self. Your empathy will be accurate and attuned to the mode in which the other person is thinking, and your openness will be genuine. It will be without hidden needs. You will be firm enough in your helping to stop destructive actions or support the forces that stop them, and to treat the causes by giving the love supplies troubled people need. And when you see people misunderstanding your love giving, you will tell them and help them to realize their error, and then help them to let the real human love in, if possible. If not, you will leave them alone.

You will become the good parent to yourself you may not have had and will teach others how to do it, and for the right reasons. This is not for any need to be needed in order to prove your own worth to your doubting negative self, but because real love flows without compulsion and without anxiety from your beautiful real self.

Chapter Seven
Love Supplies
from Within

Remember the Fourth of July sparklers that flare into dazzling brightness when they are held long enough next to an already lit sparkler? After they are lit, they burn completely on their own. These sparklers are like our real self. We don't need to be dependent on other people for love supplies forever, just until we can be filled up or lit up with enough unconditional love to the point of allowing our real self to grow strong and be able to handle most of the jobs of life.

The real self can then provide its own love supplies and nurture others.

Once a person's real self is strong, he or she has limitless amounts of love resources. Believing and cherishing your own beautiful spirit self fills up a love bucket that never runs dry. This is called emotional independence as opposed to co-dependence.

The last chapter discussed ways of receiving love supplies from others. Other people are not the only source of love. *One of the two greatest sources of love* for a real self is itself. For some people, the metaphor of having a wise, all-knowing adult self and a wonderful child real self is very useful. The wounded child self is the emotionally malnourished side of each inner child of the past, waiting for the proper love supplies to grow. The wise all-knowing adult is the part of each person that knows what our little real self child missed and helps provide the love supplies to the little child in each person through visualizations, letters, drawings, and talks where the adult real self loves and takes care of the wounded child real self.

An example might be forming a picture in your mind of a small lonely, crying child, and then using the power of your real self through visualizing a wise, all-knowing, loving adult walk into that picture with the small child and comfort it by hugging and praising her, thus providing love supplies for personal growth through the use of your own adult real self's internal resources.

The other love resource is God. Think back to the list of favorite love supplies near the beginning of Chapter Five. The fourth one, privacy and trust, can be a love supply from oneself or from God. This is time alone to think things through, to meditate and pray. This is a marvelous resource for a more mature real self. Having God or your Higher Power help the person you love—your inner child—is even better. And going by a pre-earth life self-concept where we were raised by heavenly parents is the ultimate love source.

Rescuing Your Inner Child

Our inner child of the past is within each one of us. He is far more real than any negative self lie, and yet many people refuse to believe in this wonder child. This child real self (CRS) at birth wanted only to be loved and valued for what and who he is. Children are "ninety" per cent feelings and "ten" per cent performance. Most adults don't understand this and begin to systematically dishonor this feeling identity seed and brainwash the child away from his/her true identity as a feeling being into a performance robot.

This little child is so precious, so loving, and so desirous of treatment to match her or his feeling identity that most people weep openly when they are first reintroduced and reunited with this wonder child. Why is the child hidden from our view and our conscious awareness? Her feelings were not honored, valued, respected, believed, in or understood. This sent that child's real self into hiding.

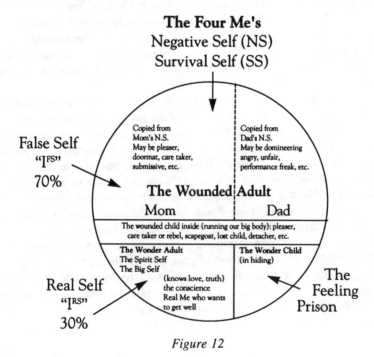

The Four Me's
Negative Self (NS)
Survival Self (SS)

False Self
"FS"
70%

Copied from Mom's N.S. May be pleaser, doormat, care taker, submissive, etc.

Copied from Dad's N.S. May be domineering angry, unfair, performance freak, etc.

The Wounded Adult
Mom   Dad

The wounded child inside (running our big body): pleaser, care taker or rebel, scapegoat, lost child, detacher, etc.

The Wonder Adult
The Spirit Self
The Big Self
(knows love, truth)
the conscience
Real Me who wants
to get well

The Wonder Child
(in hiding)

Real Self
"RS"
30%

The
Feeling
Prison

Figure 12

When the child is newborn, he desires full bodily involvement, such as skin contact by being held, cuddled, nursed, and by being one physically and emotionally with its mother. When this does not happen, he cries. Weeping is another *full* body gratification. It greatly relieves and expresses the child's true *feeling* center or core. His/her most precious part of being is here. Crying is so healthy, so real, so essential to our being who we are that no one can ever be real or progress in life without it.

When parents *shame* crying and openly or covertly shut up the little child's intense, full-body expression, which is crying, the child may become *angry*. Anger is good as long as it doesn't harm others. A child must have a safe place to express anger and not be hit for it or allowed to hurt others with it.

Parents who model getting anger out privately and honestly go far in nourishing the child's true feeling identity seed. When full-body physical and emotional affection is prevented, crying is unsafe or prevented, and anger is denied, then the unfortunate wonder child goes into hiding and a wounded child, a mutation, emerges. Copying the negative false self styles of parents and older siblings, teachers and friends happens. This child seeks full-body involvement reminiscent of the child union with the nursing mother and the hugging, holding, rocking father. In this process they seek food, drugs, sex, and a host of other substitute love supplies through bodily turn-ons. The wounded child copies parents and its styles become its wounded adult or false self, and this runs the body.

When we learn to get in touch with this hidden child and nurture her with our adult real self or wonder adult, a powerful and rapid change may take place.

Many wonderful recent publications are available for you to read to help and guide you in the recovery, helping, and rescuing of your inner child. Basically, they consist of contacting that precious being by:

1. Writing letters and drawing pictures.
2. Talking out loud and silently using a symbol of that child, such as a doll, teddy bear or photograph of your own self as a toddler or preschooler.
3. Doing visualizations, meditations, or hypnosis.

When we write a letter to our inner child, we write with our dominant hand, which is the right for most of us. By doing this we invite the child to share his feelings, with us. We may apologize for going into hiding or abandoning him, and we promise to love and honor all these feelings such as to hold, hug, kiss, praise, and support his being unconditionally. The first letter I ever wrote went something like this.

Dear Little Sterling,

I am your big self from the future. I love you so much. I miss you. I'm not real without you. Please forgive me for leaving you so long ago. Try once again to share all your feelings with me, and I promise to cherish them. I'm waiting for your reply.

Love, Big Sterling.

Then I took the pen in my *left* hand to answer back from my child of the past. It was very awkward. And as the child wrote and I later read it aloud, I wept with the intensity of pain, disappointment, and agony of the precious, beautiful, little toddler that he was. He was being treated horribly foreign to his true feeling identity.

That child in me wrote back, "I hurt inside. They don't like me. No matter how hard I try, they just don't like me. They pull my hair, my ears, and slap my face. Why don't they like me? Can you help me? Love, Li'l Sterling."

Can you feel the pain and anguish of such a precious little creature whose identity is being squashed daily? As time went on, I would send back letters of intense *love supplies* to him. The next letter from my big self said the following:

Dear Li'l Sterling,

It hurts to be slapped and pushed and pulled, doesn't it? And so embarrassing [empathy] that I can feel your pain. You can use my big self's body to cry through. I love your feelings. They are so precious to me [verbal affection]—that you may go ahead and cry all you want. Crying is good [explaining and permission].

I'm holding you on my lap right now. You feel so good to me, so soft and warm [physical affection]. Don't believe those people that hurt you. You are a wonderful li'l boy, and I will protect you from them. When you are ready, you can come up to the future and live with me forever. Tell me more about your feelings. Your pain, anger, and fear are very important to me.

Love, Big Sterling

He wrote back how much he loved my letter and that he felt better. I have written dozens of such letters to him and he to me.

All little children also love to draw. Sooner or later, some sick person in their false self will criticize our drawings, and the little child will stop drawing or painting entirely. This happens as the child's feelings are shamed and squashed, and *performance,* worshipped by adults, replaces *feelings.* No longer can he use drawing or painting to express his feelings.

Recovering that child may include your big self asking your inner child to draw himself, that is, to draw his anger, pain, fear, or whatever. These techniques are avenues to our subconscious where the little child or "record keeper" lives within. This is where he has been a prisoner for so long. All adults who still have their inner child in this prison will fight tooth and nail to put and keep your child in this prison. Why? It scares their adult, wounded, negative self because your inner child is surfacing and theirs cannot. Be ready for these negative people to attack and thwart you, and mock and shame you in every way for doing inner child discovery and reunion.

Talking with your inner child is a great thrill. In the old days, "sick" people used say, "Only crazy people talk to themselves." Not so. Today healthy people talk to themselves. You can't heal what you can't feel. Talking to your inner child is a must. It is also a great treat because you love him so much.

When I first talked to my little boy, he couldn't say his Rs very well. I was so surprised. I cried a lot. I used my older body to express his feelings of pain, anger, and fear. Now, years after, I make sure I talk with him every spare minute because I love him more than anything. I can't love anyone else until I love him—"Love thy neighbor as *thyself.*"

Especially important are our childhood repeats. Every time I'm in my false self, I ask my inner child if anything like this has ever happened to us before. He always tells me how it is a general repeat of certain childhood events and survival styles, such as living in a dysfunctional family. When I pour in the love supplies to him and get my symbol of him, such as my doll, picture, stuffed animal, or whatever, he soon feels so much better. This stops my negative self from ruling my body in the present. Try it. I hope it works as well for you.

My little boy loves physical affection, and without my physical symbol of him, I cannot give him as much good and wonderful holding, kissing, stroking, and skin-to-skin contact.

Your negative self will say, "It's so stupid. It's all imaginary. You can't go back in time like this."

I say, "Why not?" It is the most powerful, effective work I've ever done in my life for helping myself and being of help to others. Consider how imaginary your negative self is and how you let it go completely unquestioned and give it so much energy.

The idea or metaphor of *two selves* gives great clarity and ease of understanding to those of us doing personal therapy or counseling. *It is also very, very important in doing inner child work.* Some books of instruction in inner child work have no concept of the two selves and this causes patients to become very confused when the adult negative self (wounded adult) starts to trick or "beat up" the wounded child. If we were made by our parents to tend *their* feelings, when we were small, before we know it, in writing to the little child our adult negative—identified with our parent's negative self—begins to *tend* us, the big self. The wounded child of the past is confused, hurt, angry and soon stops writing and/or the patient says, "This doesn't work!"

Simply put, the solution is to *never* let your adult negative self interact with the wounded child in the writing, drawing, talking or visualizing activities. If your "parent-taught adult negative self" does creep in, as soon as you recognize it (it will have styles just like your parents did), say to your little child, "a monster has me; don't pay any attention! It's not the good big me you trust and love."

Immediately protect your inner child from this "bad big self" and get on track again with the good big self giving the love supplies to the wounded child of the past.

You may need to explain the two big selves to the inner child sometime. He will understand all too well.

Other ways this can happen is when patients say, "I can't give love to this little child, I'm way too sick (depressed, empty, etc.) to do this." Or, "I hate that little brat! I'll scratch his eyes out." This is clearly an example of "identification with the abusers" (parent's negative self). The "I" referred to is the adult negative self. It has the same contempt for the inner child as our parents had for us! Or, it has the same attitude of being overwhelmed, too busy to bother, neglect, etc. that our parents had for us. When this happens and goes unchecked, the inner child work will surely fail, if not at first, eventually this is certain. Some patients often ask, "Who is the big good self? I don't feel it. I can't do it."

Which self are they calling "I?" The adult (parent-taught) negative self. The "big good self" is the same part of them that brought them to therapy. The self that's looking to heal is the one we are looking for. Every part of us that wants to heal, that makes the sacrifice to come to therapy, to read this book, to help our children or our marriage, is powerful evidence that we do have a "big good self" inside.

The therapist's big good self must also be a tender but powerful ally to the patient who feels this way. Constant therapist love supplies to the struggling patient, over time, will triumph. Soon the patient's big (or not so big) good self will grow and nourish the wounded child back to health and to a merger with the wonder child and wonder adult. BE CAREFUL. If it doesn't work, don't always blame the instrument, look at the user as well.

Time is a learning device. It isn't a big deal to the real self. If the false self can say that time is nothing and all that happened to you in childhood can run your adult life just as if time didn't count, then why can't real self say that time is nothing. This means we can go back and let the present heal the past and bring the inner child into alignment with the adult self. You have to want to cherish the scared wounded child in you.

You can go back as easily as you can go forward. Time is part of this Earth School and it is reversible. This is more clearly seen in meditations, visualizations, and self-hypnosis, which is the third way of loving and reuniting with your child real self and healing the wounded child. This takes away his wounds and scars of past mistreatment and allows us to be real, possessing all of our child's vitality, enthusiasm, optimism, curiosity, and zest for living, growing, learning, and loving.

Some of the books for doing inner child work have printed word-by-word meditations in them which you can tape record in your own voice with soft, relaxing music for each stage of life: infancy, toddler, preschool, school age, and adolescence. These hypnotic exercises can go a long, long way in loving and reuniting you with your inner child.

My own four visualization tapes, as well as many others, are a great asset in rescuing your little child from the feeling prison. Group work as well with a safe partner makes this love for your inner child even more powerful for all. Try it.

Often people wonder about visualization accurately revealing past events, especially sexual and physical abuse. The major reason to do visualizations is to give the child of the past love supplies, not to discover past real events.

Several studies show how easy it is with some people to hypnotize them into believing real lies about their past. Beware of therapists with unfinished business of their own. They may need you to discover something to fill *their* unmet needs. This is why I urge you to do your own visualizations as soon as you can. No competent therapist would ever urge any patient to legally prosecute another because in a dream or visualization they "found out" they were abused. Therapists are not lawyers. Dreams and hypnosis often come in symbols and not always in external reality. Your job is healing the child, *not revenge.*

It is fully possible for us to heal very well in this work and never mention it to our parents. Think of all the patients whose parents are dead. They fully recover from abuse. So can you.

Many of my clients have seen, as well as I have, that doing this inner child "work," (which in reality is play), changes their perception and relationship to all other physical children, meaning their own as well as others.

We begin to speak more kindly, softly, politely to them. We see through their eyes. We hug them more, use praise, and honor their beings and feelings. Then their performances flow, just as surely as the caboose follows the engines of a great long train. As we love our own inner child so preciously, tenderly, and carefully, so we begin to love all other children. They are not our slaves, our egos, our property, our reputation. They are valuable, independent, feeling, thinking beings whose identity needs must be met, or they will mutate and become performance robots. In short, rebels and pleasers. Their souls will be "murdered" by our false selves.

So many children fear death, abandonment, even tell stories about little children being killed, eaten, maimed, and so on. These may be re-enactment in fantasy of their own inner child's near death or imprisonment in the feeling prison. Adults, too, have the compulsion to repeat their own helplessness and escape it by identifying with their feeling abusers to get power from this near death of their inner child. They avoid feelings like the plague and worship their performance and appearance gods.

When we wake up and begin to realize that feelings are far more important than performances, false wounded selves will impose "feeling stoppers" to us. They say, "Don't *dwell* on that; it's done. You can't change the past. Forget it and get on with your life." Or "Quit blaming your parents," or "Are you going to keep those feelings the rest of your life?" or "When will you stop all this crying and anger?" and so on. They go *assuming* that feelings are bad and they won't "get you anywhere," which means worldly success and performance.

It was not our fault that our parents were in their false survival selves when we were little and helpless beings, even though it has crippled us for years. It *is* our fault now if we don't do something about it. Jesus said, "Ye shall know the truth, and the truth shall make you free."

The feeling truth will free you forever to be what you really are to be. It will be painful at first. It always is. But all of us must taste the bitter to prize the sweet. Persevere—it is worth it!

Now let's move on to other similar forms of love supplies from ourselves. Inner child work is not the only way to receive love supplies from yourself.

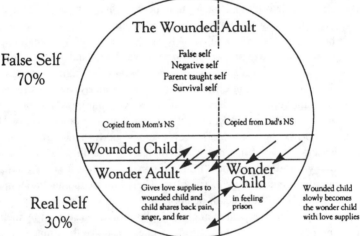

Inner Child Work Diagram
(Four "selves" repaired)

Figure 13

Other Meditations and Pondering

People often admire and love character traits they see in others, yet never recognize that they possess these same character traits themselves. They miss a chance to give themselves valuable love supplies. However, if they will use meditation, which is thinking and feeling intensely while the external world is shut out, they can begin to recognize some of these same deep feelings and internal qualities which give evidence of their own real self inside. Sometimes in our fondest desires, intense positive yearnings, and long-term goals, we experience evidences of our real self.

In order to use meditation to get in touch with you real self, you need to set aside some quiet time. This is best done on a daily basis, but you can have a marvelous experience even doing it just once.

Begin by telling yourself—your inside, your beautiful, spirit self that knows many, many things and can feel deeply and know how to love fully—that you want some specific thing. Focus on a character trait that you would like to own. This can be something that perhaps you admire in others, that is, if you can't think of one you already possess. Learn to recognize that trait in yourself and fall in love with it. Admire it in yourself. Seriously dwell upon the thing. Own it. Put it foremost in your mind and think of your beautiful real self as already having it.

This way your real self can better emerge. Use all the tricks that your false self uses to flow so easily, only now do it for your real self.

Many individuals are afraid of and alarmed by their negative thoughts. This alarm and fear gives energy to their false self and much more negative power. We cannot shut up the negative self; it is part of our Earth School experience to try us and test us and thus refine us like precious gold and strengthen our real self. One way we win over the negative self is by giving equal energy and attention to the *positive* versions of our thoughts, just as alarm and fear are energy to the negative. We do not put perfume over garbage. Those who do are sick. The false self is real, but it is only a learning device. It is not our true identity.

When this does not work and a negative avalanche covers us, then we need to go deeper and deeper and feel the feelings, as in garbage dumping, or doing the three questions,
or finishing sentences to find our wounds and frustrated expectations.

In focusing on a character trait, one person might discover his great love and respect for a friend, or he might begin to sense his own ability to feel with others what they are feeling. This helps to gain empathy. He might learn to recognize his courage, loyalty, persistence, desire to grow, or sensitivity, all of which are evidences of his real self. These traits are not originally taught by anyone else; they flow from his deep, inner self. When this person actually recognizes the marvelous traits of his real self, he is thrilled and awed to own them. "It's ME!" one patient exclaimed. This is always a very positive and deeply moving experience. It is never negative. It is never used to impress other, but instead is totally private and sacred. It serves forever as a great anchor during bad storms. One of the best references on this matter is Gendlin's book, *Focusing*, where he takes you through six steps. He has you close your eyes and go through them, stopping whenever you need to. Try it.

People who use their visual modes a lot often see a mental picture of their real self. One woman saw a beautiful white flower like a lily unfolding slowly; then out of that flower grew up another identical one, which opened and brought forth another and then another, until there was a tall tower of beautiful white flowers, each within another, reaching up to the clouds. Similarly, people who most often use their kinesthetic or auditory modes will *feel* or *hear* some wonderful representation of their real self.

As you sit alone in silence and learn to sense some of the beautiful, positive character traits that are truly a part of you, you gain a wonderful resource. Treasuring these traits can be like treasuring precious jewels, taking them out of their hiding place any time you want to look at them. Realizing that you own these beautiful qualities and experiencing the feeling of "That's me" allows you to become tremendously more independent emotionally. You don't always need to be told of your fine qualities; you will sense them privately within yourself. You can feel good about yourself, even when no one else seems to be noticing you.

Neither do you need to worry about so many of the little criticisms, failures, and ups and downs of life, or about what others think. What they think about is them, not you, and comes from *their* own childhood. It is none of *your* affair.

You are internally independent, and this independence gives power to the real self and comes from the real self. It has no need to seek for love or to take anything from other. It is not lured by any of the false illusions of "love" that the world offers, which are cheap substitutes. And this identity independence is permanent. No one can take it away. No prison can lock it up, no series of performances, good or bad, can ruin it. It is true, and no failure, mistake, or success can touch it. No one else has power over it. No amount of abuse can permanently destroy it.

It is uniquely, independently yours. And as you discover the truth about your real self and sense your general sameness with all other human beings, as well as your complete specific uniqueness, the greater your love becomes for yourself and for others. You become more open in loving others and more open to the greater love that can come from God, who is our real self source.

Reshaping the Past

Another way people can give themselves love supplies is by learning to use their new-found, real-self resources to deal with hurtful situations from the past. They can actually recreate their history by imagining how things might have been, using their real selves instead of their negative selves to resolve old problems.

One man I was working with did this very successfully by using an imaginary time tunnel. He was still bothered and hurt by something that had happened to him many years before. So I asked him to close his eyes, go into his time tunnel, and go back until he came to his big hurt, then stop. When he did, I could see the pain all over his face. He waited there for a minute, re-experiencing the hurt. Then I asked him to slide back up in time to the present moment and find something from his real self which he could take back there to help him. He consulted with his present-day real self and found some special traits or assets he could use in the hurtful situation, a love supply he hadn't possessed at the time the incident happened. He took that resource back into the time tunnel, went back to the painful memory, and relived the hurtful situation, this time turning the event over to his real self, with new love supplies. When he finished, he relaxed his whole body, smiled all over, and opened his eyes. He felt happy, successful, and more capable as a result of having imagined a new experience to replace the old one. This is very much like inner-child work visualization. For a good reference on this method, read Cameron-Bandler, *They Lived Happily Ever After* (pages 109-117). This is an excellent example of how it works.

This type of exercise can probably be even more effective if you are able to create a mental picture of yourself as you go through it. Test yourself right now to see how well you can visualize. Stare at a nearby object for several minutes, then close your eyes and create a visual picture of that same object in your mind. Most people can do this. With practice, almost everyone can do it very well. Next, try to make other objects appear in your mind's eye at will. As you do this, try to see yourself sitting just as you are right now, as though you were looking at yourself from above or from across the room. At first your mental "picture" may have vague outlines or lack details, but that's all right. The details will fill in as you practice.

Now, to use this visualizing technique to help clear up unpleasant negative events from the past, you should first relax. Sit or lie down in a relaxed position and, after closing your eyes, "see" yourself in a recent situation where you handled things very well, one in which you were very satisfied with yourself. See yourself in a situation where you were strict and firm, yet kind and understanding. In other words, during a time when your real self was in charge.

Let all the powerful feelings you had then of peace, harmony, and strength wash over you again. As these wonderful feelings fill you and you can clearly "see" the situation—perhaps "hear" the voices from it as well—squeeze your right leg, somewhere on the knee or thigh, as a reminder of or an anchor for the real self's demonstration.

Now, let the vision fade, and in a minute or two, remember and visualize another situation. See yourself in a past situation in which your negative self was in charge. Notice the unders or overs style of your negative self and its other characteristics. As you feel again all the frustrated, upset, angry or helpless feelings you felt then, squeeze your left knee or thigh, making it your negative "anchor" signal. Then in a moment, squeeze the left leg again, bringing back the bad feelings, and at the same time squeeze your right leg or thigh in the same way as before. Be sure to imitate exactly your earlier squeezing. This can bring back the memory of the real-self resource experience and all of its positive strength and power; then you'll "see" and feel or hear your real self taking over and cleaning up the negative situation.

Stick with this until the real self triumphs. Once you have done this and realize how much better you feel afterward, you can use this same procedure as a powerful love supply any time you need it. Go all the way back to your early childhood if necessary, to negative experiences at ages 4, 5, and 6; then squeeze your real-self resource signal to bring all your adult power and strength to the situation. Doing this every day will bring you the best results, but no matter how often you do it, you'll find the memory of your experiences completely changed once you have turned them over to your real self.

There are two reasons why this procedure actually changes past experiences. First, in the relaxed mental state of a good visualization, time does not exist, at least not in the same way that we know it consciously. So what you remember as happening "back then" is as real and as much present as what happens today. You can slide back and forth mentally in time to deal with any situation you want to. Secondly, it isn't the actual event from the past that hurts so much as it is the way we are thinking about it now, in the present. If we can change the memory of a past event, we in effect change its hurting potential. This is so because what really haunts us is the *way we remember the event*, not necessarily the way it really was. Letting the real self, with all its marvelous strength, take over a memory that our negative self has previously handled makes the outcome totally different. We feel successful and confident. Anyone whose childhood was full of negative experiences still has those painful memories, but with this visualization procedure they can be rebuilt into real-self resources. And that will greatly improve the present. Read Bry's book, *Visualizations*, or *Frogs and Princes* by Bandler, or Grinder's already mentioned.

Another way you can draw on real-self resources when your negative self seems to be too overpowering is to simply relax physically, then mentally take yourself back to one of your happiest times in the past. Perhaps to yesterday or go as far back as you wish. Relive that time very slowly, or else over and over, in your mind. This reliving can give you added real self resources to draw on in difficult times.

The same kind of visualization procedure can be used for future events. If you foresee a situation coming up in which you would typically revert to your negative self and come out feeling bad, you can prepare for it. Visualize yourself in that future situation, this time using the new resource or love supply from your real self. Squeeze your resource anchor and watch your own mental movie of how your real self can create a desirable outcome instead of an unhappy one. After doing this you'll be much more able to act with your real-self resources. Instead of using negative-self substitutes, you will overcome these negative forces.

When the situation does come along, be wise and alert. If it doesn't work, turn to the chapter that deal with catharsis emotionally, verbally, and physically dealing with crying, screaming, and hitting. Then return to these visualization treats. They will work better.

Thought Detection and Thought Selection—
A cognitive Approach

Our thoughts can come mostly from our real selves, or they can come mostly from our negative selves. Therefore, thoughts can provide good, real-love supplies, or they can provide cheap substitutes. If only we could choose our thoughts so that we nearly always got the truth, what a powerful resource we would possess! It is possible. It will take time and great commitment, but it really is possible. This is a powerful resource we could implement into our daily lives and make us humbly supreme within.

To use this love resource requires that we first learn to carefully notice our thoughts and feelings that accompany it. To identify where our thoughts are coming from is the first step. This can take a good deal of effort and concentration on our part at first. You must be open and sensitive to your insides.

Suppose as a parent that you had this thought: *I did the right thing when I reminded Suzie of her chores without raising my voice.* That's a nice thought, don't you think? Then you think future, *I'm learning to handle this type of situation better.* This is positive, real-self thinking. Excellent.

Then comes this thought, *I blew it this morning. Even though I didn't raise my voice at Suzie, I still wanted to yell like thunder. I guess I'll never learn how to discipline the children in the right way.*

First, remember that this kind of negative thinking comes from the false, negative self. But what do the two types of thought, one the real self thinking and the other the negative self thinking imply? The first implies that this mother is capable at heart, able to learn and grow and gradually master new skills. The second pushes her down by implying that she may never learn completely. She decides that she is basically inferior or inadequate in some way. This hurts her identity. It is a lie.

The kind of thoughts that come from our negative selves don't match our true identities. Face it, they are lies. They are cheap substitutes for the real love that we can give ourselves when we discover thoughts that do match our true identities. These cheap substitute thoughts can eventually become so deeply ingrained that they become the fully developed, negative cover-ups that we talked about in Chapter Three.

The substitute thought says, *I'm the only one who knows anything around here.* This is a superior or bossiness cover-up. *I'm the one who always has to suffer. Poor me.* This becomes a martyr cover-up; and so on.

However, when we learn to detect these kinds of thoughts, and when we consciously choose to own other thoughts more consistent with our true identities, then we begin to give power to our real selves as we take it away from our false self that is accustomed to surviving in a toxic past.

Sometimes it's hard to detect which source or self a thought is coming from. The obviously negative thoughts are easy to trace, such as, "I'm a clumsy fool." We know which self that comes from.

But what about this thought? *I mustn't tell Mark that I'm disappointed in the way he seemed to ignore my feelings, because he might be hurt and upset,* thinks Judy. Did he, in fact, ignore her feelings? It could be her wrong interpretation of what happened.

What is so wrong about Mark being upset? He might reject her for her comment. He might leave. So what? If he rejects her, does that make her a bad person? Or might it mean that he has a problem? All of these questions may be rolling around in her head. The implication is that Judy is not a lovable person unless others like and approve of her. This is not so. These kinds of thought are sometimes hard to identify as coming from the negative or real self.

Others have struggled with this issue of which is which. Some excellent reading is Bandler and Grinder's, *The Structure of Magic,* Volume I.

Part of the key to thought detection and thought selection is realizing that *we* choose our thoughts. We may have learned to think in certain ways from others, but we do make our own thoughts now. Therefore, we can choose to keep these thoughts or get rid of them.

Another part of the key is using the same three ingredients of real love with ourselves that we use with others:

1. Empathy.
2. Openness.
3. Firmness.

We need empathy with ourselves in order to *listen* to, or *see*, or *feel* the "thoughts" coming from both positive and negative selves. And, likewise, we need to be open to all our thoughts. We must allow ourselves to be aware of the not-so-pleasant as well as the pleasant ones. If we hide or repress them, we'll never be able to get control over them.

The third ingredient, firmness, is needed to exercise thought control, when we choose to disown a negative-self thought and own a real-self thought. This can be very, very difficult if we are in the habit of doing just the opposite, such as using our real self to be with our negative self. Working with thoughts is cognitive and superficial. Working with feelings is deeper and more complete, but more difficult.

How to Do It

Let's look at this process of thought detection and thought selection in more detail. First, we have to use empathy and openness to identify our thoughts. If we wish to notice a negative inner voice, we do it with our auditory mode. If we feel the negative, then it is with our kinesthetic mode, and to receive the negative picture we have our visual mode. Whatever mode we use, it is essential that we note what our reaction is during these first thoughts. Think about it. Does this thought give you a feeling of being little, silly, stupid, incapable, or bumbling? Does the thought give you a good feeling about yourself, such as peacefulness, confidence, or self-esteem?

The attitude of concentration on our thoughts requires observing, listening, and checking our feelings. Be very alert to thoughts running through the mind. Thoughts follow each other so fast that it's easy, especially when we allow our thoughts free rein, to wind up with a bad feeling and not to have even noticed how we brought it on. Our brains that are magnificently complex, much like a supercomputer, are easily able to monitor all of this, but most of us are not used to making our brain work for us in this special way. We think it is too difficult, or our negative self tells us it is not worth it or essential to getting on with life. It is very essential. It may be the very core of your future happiness.

Some patients say to me, "Dr. Ellsworth, since I have been coming to you, I have nothing but headaches from thinking constantly about my thoughts."

Okay. I know that in the beginning some people get headaches. This is to be expected. It is hard work to begin sorting thoughts if you are not in training for such an exercise. Jogging is difficult for the beginner, sore muscles and all. This is the nature of things in body and mind. Keep it up. Eventually, with practice, the build-up comes. Like jogging, you reach the training effect, and you have the wind to go long distances with some ease. The same thing is true of sorting thoughts and making them work for you.

Once you develop working with your thoughts and have done it regularly, it will surprise you how well you can do this, and without pain. The end goal is happiness. Why not have a minigoal tomorrow or next week that you will work at it so diligently that you will accelerate your mental conditioning so that in a matter of days you will begin to feel that you have reached a level of little pain. If you work your brain about thoughts as well as most people work up until they can jog easily, you will be a much happier person, more intelligent, much more aware, and more loving than ever before. It's up to you.

After identifying thoughts that have come from the false self, call for your real-self version. If that seems too hard at first, just think of the exact opposite thought from the original negative one. Give your real self equal time on the television of your mind.

You must now own and reinforce the positive thoughts you have. If you need more help hearing what your real self has to say, you can ask others who know your real self to help you. Make your friends allies in your war against your negative self. Let them help you find the real-self resource which can counter negative thoughts. You'll find that exposing your negative self to them will help you see how silly and weak it really is. Nothing takes the power out of a negative thought quite like exposing it to the light where safe people can see it. You'll watch it quickly wither and die because it's a fake, false, unreal thing. It's necessary only to test you and help you grow. It thrives only in the dark, among the stupid or in the unknown.

The next step is often the hardest, and that is making your mind and body obey your real self instead of your false self. This takes real firmness. You actually need to kick out the thoughts that come from your negative self. This can be very, very difficult, this so partly because this firmness is hard to distinguish from negative-self forms of repression and suppression that psychologists call *denial*.

For example, if I say I really didn't have negative thoughts in the first place, I am just hiding them from my own awareness. This keeps me from understanding how they work and leaves me helpless in dealing with them. It also produces psychosomatic symptoms because the negative thoughts won't go away. They just fester beneath the surface. Denial, then, is simply denying that negative thoughts exist. Instead, go ahead and acknowledge negative thoughts; learn all about them. You must know them to fight them. The old saying "Knowledge is power" was never more true. This kind of power is what is needed to understand the real self. Finishing sentences about negative self style pay offs can bring alarming insights.

Sometimes we need to use all of our firmness to put the negative thoughts out and put thoughts that match our true identity in place. We cannot simply throw the negative ones away and leave an empty place. Nothing cannot replace something. We may need to force ourselves to look for the good in others. This is not to say that we give false praise, but look deeply for the real value that all humans possess by nature. Even our trying to grow and find joy is a sign of our good self.

One lady said to me, "My mind is like a brown paper bag; it has all sorts of thoughts in it. When a thought comes out, I look at it and say, 'Does that thought match the noble and true identity of my real self?' If it doesn't, then I say to my brain, 'Brain, I do not want that false thought. Throw it out. Get rid of it. Erase it from my brain. What else do you have in there? Do you have a thought that matches my true identity?'"

Of course there are thoughts to match our best self. What a great way to do positive thoughts. But be careful of lying to yourself and covering pain and anger with Pollyanna positivism. It won't work. It could do damage.

Thoughts Can Progress to Acts

For some people, thoughts seem to come first, then feelings; after that words, then acts. In others feelings precede thoughts, then acts. If you leave a thought from your negative self unchecked, it produces a negative feeling and vice versa. So you feel inadequate, stupid, or unlovable. After a while, if you allow yourself to have lots of these feelings, your words will begin to reflect them. You'll degrade yourself and others; perhaps you will say that you or someone else is not smart or capable or friendly. After enough of these kinds of remarks, your actions will be affected. You will do things that hurt your body, such as drinking, drugs—you name it.

In time you will begin associating with persons who will put you down. Your negative self will progressively get control of your thoughts, then your feelings, next your words, and finally your actions. Before long they have all of you. You become just one large, negative person.

Because of this progression, it is much easier to detect and select thoughts than to wait. This way you avoid negative acts. They are so hard to live with. Still in all, negative thoughts are small compared to negative acts. This is where people really get into trouble. For some, it costs them their very lives.

A small fire in the corner of the kitchen is relatively easy to dowse, but if you wait until after it has spread to the living room and on to the bedroom, it takes the whole house with it.

This chart on *Thought Detection and Thought Selection* shows how little thoughts or feelings, positive or negative, can spread into action. They do grow.

Thought Detection and Thought Selection

Negative Self	Body	Positive Self
- thoughts 100 NGU	brain	+ thoughts 100 PGU
- feelings 200 NGU	"heart"	+ feelings 200 PGU
- words 300 NGU	mouth	+ words 300 PGU
- acts 400 NGU	whole body	+ acts 400 PGU

NGU = negative growth units   PGU = positive growth units

The body is in the middle. It is the great prize that positive and negative selves compete to control. And the numbers in either column are imaginary nutrients called "growth units."

Now, suppose you have a positive thought, one coming from your real self, such as, *I'm a helpful, kind person.* At that moment, your positive self is controlling your brain, and your real self is being fed because it is in charge. It is handling the jobs of life for you. So this gets a hundred positive growth units (PGU). When that thought progresses to a feeling about yourself such as, *I'm good and I'm lovable,* your real self gets two hundred positive growth units because feelings are more powerful than thoughts. Plus, your real self controls more of your body. It affects your heart and brain.

A little later, when you speak positively and honestly, you strengthen your real self even more with three hundred new positive growth units, and your real self gets control of still more of you. The final step is to act from your real self: *do the right thing for the right reason.*

Help a friend, compile a report, drive an elderly woman to the store. This helps you actualize your own loving self. When your real self has control of your whole body, you will act, speak, feel, and think in accordance with this true noble identity. *You'll do right things for the right reasons.* Keep this in your waking thoughts; it is so important. It keeps you in touch with your real self.

Now, while all this is going on, your negative self is probably working overtime, vying with your real self for control of your body. On the ground level, it is submitting thoughts that contradict your true identity. Such things will pop up as this, *Listen to that foolish remark you made. She's going to think you have no manners.* What you do with these negative thoughts makes a big difference.

If they are louder than the positive thoughts, since your negative self has been getting more exercise over the years, you'll either have to consciously throw them out or accept them. If you accept them, your negative self gets a hundred negative growth units. This is like counting cancer cells in the body. Pretty soon you'll have some negative feelings and then perhaps some negative words, then actions will take over, and your negative self hogs more and more negative units.

If, on the other hand, your positive thoughts are drowning out the negative ones, because your real self has grown bigger and stronger than your negative, you'll be able to simply ignore the negative thoughts; they'll fade away. Whichever self is getting exercised the most is the one that gets the growth units. It's a fact of living in the Earth School. This is learning being tested.

Remember that one key to helping your real self win the struggle is detecting feelings and thoughts. If you can't catch your thoughts, try to be very aware of what kind of feelings you are having. But please don't wait for words or actions. Catch your negatives as quickly as you can. Be firm with these destructive thoughts. They are important. Winning over the lying self is major. Learning how is a device so you won't die dumb.

**Dumping Your Own Garbage—
a Feeling Approach**
Real selves are a lot like engines in cars or other machines. They don't work very well when they get covered with sludge. Oil, dirt, and grime dirty engines. Likewise, if we collect and hold on to anger and pain from past experiences, it accumulates psychological sludge, emotional garbage, which covers the real self and keeps it from working efficiently.

All of us do this occasionally. In spite of our best efforts, we may believe and absorb negative comments or implications about ourselves made by someone else's negative self. And sometimes we take in lies without realizing it because we are caught by surprise. Each of these lies forms a thin layer of sludge, and after collecting several layers, our emotional engines choke and sputter with pain and resentful anger.

How can we know when we have a lot of emotional garbage that needs to be dumped? What are the signs that will help us recognize a need to clean up? One way that pain resulting from built-up sludge and garbage starts to show is that we get grumpy or grouchy, angry or aggressive. Hostility and touchiness come into play as well. We are quick to speak sharply or to use a mean tone of voice, or just plain sad much of the time.

These signs mean that our garbage is getting close to the surface and it's time to get rid of it. Sometimes, though, before we even notice these symptoms, we discover that for some reason our thought detection and thought selection process isn't working.

It seems that all the instructions and the recipes that have worked so well in the past—all the positive thinking and thought control—no longer works. This is usually the first indication that the real self is getting clogged up with layers of garbage, lies, and misinformation from the false self. We appear to be inefficient, sluggish, and weak. We need to pump some life back into our real self.

There are many ways to dump garbage. Probably the most popular and easiest way is to pour it out verbally to a kind and understanding friend. Select someone who can give pure empathy and who makes it safe for you to share your pain and anger. These kinds of people can be found. They don't confuse your garbage with your real self. The trouble is that these kinds of friends are *very rare*. Perhaps five to ten per cent of the people at best Most people don't have them immediately available. You can tell who they are.

Ways to Dump

So it is very important to dump your *own* garbage. Here are some ways that work for people who are ready to do it.

Journaling

l. Writing works very well for some people. They get great relief by writing angry feelings in a "garbage" journal or letter. This is best written as if you are telling this to a friend you trust.

Dream Work

2. Writing down dreams is the same kind of strategy. In addition to providing catharsis, writing dreams can also give insights into just what kind of garbage there is inside you. Many people can't remember their dreams. These are often people who won't show openness. Interesting people. They tend not to sing, laugh, cry, pray, hug, kiss, or say they are sorry.

Their feelings are repressed. But if they will consciously try to remember even little snatches of a dream or single mental image and write it down on a pad for recall beside their bed, or as they arise in the morning, it will help focus on dreams.

Analyzing the themes of each dream, for example the overs and unders parts of negative self, can lead you to more understanding and knowledge of your negative self, and to ways of dumping more garbage.

Empty Chair — Screaming

3. Another effective way to dump garbage is to roll up your car windows, drive out on a freeway, where there are few cars near you, and yell and scream to your heart's content. This can lead to an empty chair where you pretend a person you have unfinished business with is sitting. Or, if you prefer, grab a pillow and set it on a chair and talk to it. Get all the pain and anger out in the open. Be sure to release all of your lockedup feelings of the past.

The Three Questions

4. A fourth way to dump garbage is to use a powerful technique involving questioning yourself. You can do this alone or with a trusted friend.

1. WHAT ARE YOU AWARE OF INSIDE? (This means how you feel inside.)

· Where do you feel it in your body? Point to a place such as lungs, chest, stomach, arms, legs, back, hands, shoulders, head, neck, face, eyes, throat, and mouth where he felt the most negative. These are all places where garbage can be stored, and you'll usually discover a clue to your fears when you locate the part of your body that stores the feeling. For example, a perfectionist's fear of making a mistake will often be centered in his hands where his performance could go wrong. Another person who cares immensely about how he looks might feel the feeling in his eyes. Many, many people hold tension in their stomachs, and many others in their neck and backs. Stomach means deep down and it needs to be vomited up. Neck, shoulders, back means a heavy load or burden you are carrying.

Feeling something in your lungs or chest often means you need to sigh or take a deep breath, and many people do that after they have talked or yelled or cried it up or out.

"Arms" often means something about hugs or embraces. It can also go with hands to indicate failure of a performance.

"In my heart or chest" can also mean pain of rejection or no love. Sometimes we cry as we feel this one.

"In my legs and/or feet" can mean grounded to the earth, or mobility. It can accompany positive feelings or the lack of being stable. Often the garbage comes out our eyes (tears), nose (mucous), or mouth (words, moans, screams, or crying sounds). When a person feels it in his throat, etc. you'll often see the pouring out of the stored up or frozen energy immediately thereafter.

The beauty of the three questions is that you can do them all alone. Some people are afraid of this, though, and they want someone they can trust to help them with it. Others are way too embarrassed and much prefer to do it alone. You know best what is right for you. Some say they can fix bodily aches and pains this way, too.

If you can't seem to get anywhere by asking yourself the questions, and you don't have anyone who can ask them for you, put them on a cassette tape, speaking each one ten to twenty seconds apart. Then when you are grumpy or grouchy and you need to dump garbage, turn on the tape player and you can answer the questions just as though someone else were there asking them. Try it for yourself. Now let's go on to the other two questions.

2. WHAT DO YOU WANT?

· Where do you feel this desire in your body?

3. WHAT ARE YOU AFRAID OF? As you try to isolate a specific fear, then ask:

· Where in your body do you feel that? After the third question, go back to the first and ask the three questions over and over again as fast as you can answer them. This procedure will help you get to the core of your grumpiness and sadness, and you'll find your garbage can come pouring out. And that will bring immense relief and great insight from your real self, now freer to act with the sludge removed.

It is very important in doing the three questions to repeat them over and over until you get three positive answers in a row. These answers will be something like this:

1. "How do I feel inside?" I feel better. "Where do you feel it in your body?" All over, especially in my (mentions the body part where he felt the most negative).

2. "What do you want?" I want to feel this way all the time. "Where do you feel it?" In my heart, etc. or all over.

3. "What are you afraid of?" Uhh—I'm not afraid of anything, wow!. Of course, what is there to be afraid of if you can really see things right?

"Where do you feel it?" All over, especially in my heart or chest, etc.

It is possible to finish sentences as you go, also. Combining any or all of these methods, as *you* see works best for you, is the way to go.

In this method, as in the U-turn (see chart, page 117), we want the real self (the positive) to have the last word. The aim of all these methods is love supplies from the real self.

Finishing Sentences
5. Another way to dump garbage is to describe your feelings by finishing ten sentences beginning with "I am frustrated because (or about) . . ." Use whatever word describes your emotions: frustrated, sad, angry, grouchy, upset, and so on. For example, you could begin this way: "I am sad because . . . it is so rainy and cold today." Then go on: "I am sad because . . . my kids are so mean. I am sad because . . . my husband left this morning without giving me a kiss. I just hate it when my husband leaves without giving me a kiss. He is so selfish and mean. . . . I need him so much. I wish I didn't need him so much. I don't know why I am so touchy just because he didn't give me a kiss; it ruins my whole day. I am sad because I am too dependent on him, and my life is controlled by him. I am not going to be dependent any more.

. . . I feel a lot better already seeing that I don't have to be sad just because he didn't give me a kiss."

If you find you have a lot more to say after the tenth sentence, keep right on pouring it out. There's nothing magic about the number of sentences. Ten is simply a starter. The more you can pour out, the better and the less clogged up with emotional sludge you will be.

It is also very insightful to "drill down." This means making the answer into the next stem or sentence. "I am dependent on my husband because." Take the answer and make it into a new sentence and keep going until you hit the jackpot, which is usually, "because I was brainwashed and believed lies, and now I don't anymore."

It is obvious to see that finishing sentences can bring great insight into payoffs or causes of problems or "hangups."

When a person comes to therapy, I always ask right off, "What can I help you with?" Or, "Of all the things you've been talking about, which one do you want to work on the most?" If they say, for instance, "My depression," I will often say, "Let's finish some sentences real fast and learn more about your depression. Just blurt out what comes. It doesn't have to be *right*; you can *guess*; you can even *make things up*. If you go real fast and just feel it, not think it, it will be deeper and better for you. It may bring up tears, anger, pain, or fear, but that will help the most. Here we go."

Then I will say, "I am depressed because . . ." We will do five or six of these to get some themes about their sadness and pain, which will *always* show their missing love supply—the lifeblood of their identity seed.

Often they will say something like this: "I'm depressed because I hate school," or "because I hate my job." "I'm depressed because I feel my parents (or spouse or friends) don't care about me, don't like me, don't spend time with me, are too busy, boss me around, don't listen, don't understand, don't hug, praise, etc."

Or they dwell on the symptom for which they came: "I'm depressed because I daydream, or sleep too much, or eat, or take drugs, or escape, or tried suicide, or have insomnia, headaches, care take, cry all the time, have a bad temper, tics, am shy, grouchy, critical, hit, argue, etc., etc."

Then we take the answer and go deeper. "I'm angry (shy, mean, rude, escaping, eating, sexing, etc.) because . . . . I'm not happy. I'm not living the life I wanted." (Often tears come.)

We continue. "I'm not happy because . . ." They reply: "I'm not happy because I failed in this or that," or "Someone rejected me" (by doing or saying this or that).

Then we take the sense or the feeling of that answer and make up a new sentence: "I need to succeed or have someone like me because . . ."

Usually after finishing many sentences kindly and quickly the person will say something like this, ". . . because I don't love myself—that's why I'm so dependent on and vulnerable to what happens outside of me."

This is a great insight. Then we go on. "I don't love myself because . . ." The answers are usually about childhood rejection by siblings, parents, teachers, and friends. This brainwashed them into believing they were and still are unlovable, and have to earn love or fail and die, and use all the negative-self styles and more which we have spoken of so far.

The therapist or your own real self can now say, "I believed those sick people because . . ." They often reply: "I was little; I didn't know better; I thought they were right about me." The new sentence then is, "I have to believe them forever because . . ." This is where most people say, "I don't have to believe them anymore!" I say, "I don't have to because . . ." They say, "because I know better now and I am big. I can see they are wrong and don't even know themselves. Why would I believe them anymore?"

Then the therapist or your own real self can go back to the hang-ups or symptoms or problems they came for and finish sentences about that to see how obsolete these love substitutes are now, *if* they can truly get *love supplies* into their life from God, real self, and others.

The sentences are usually something like this: "I don't have to depend on spouse's, (boss's, friend's) love anymore because . . ."; or "I don't need food, (sex, drugs, escape, success, tempers, etc.) anymore because . . ."; or finally, the big one, "I'm not depressed anymore because . . ."; or "I feel better because . . ."

It is obvious to see that such a technique has its limitations, and just because someone can logically finish these sentences doesn't make him well. But it does begin the process. In this way, 1) insight about origins can come, and 2) pain, anger, and fear can be released. We can move from conscious to subconscious if we will do these often and honestly, blurting and feeling as we go. I have been amazed at the quick progress I and many others have made in finishing sentences.

We may also collect our feelings from childhood by finishing such sentences as, "When I was little, it seemed to me that Dad (Mom) was always . . ." Finish as many as you can until you come to a blank. If your negative self says, "I don't know," your real self can say, "Just guess. You don't have to know." Or change the stem a little. "Dad or Mom was a person who . . ." When people always say only good things, then say "Sometimes Dad or Mom was . . ." Other good stems are "Dad or Mom made me feel . . . .(many times)." And "one thing I always wanted from Dad or Mom and never got, was . . ." (do five or six of these until you come to a blank). Or include such sentences as, "I resent that Dad or Mom . . . ."

These stems and many many others can help us so much to cathart and gain valuable insights, cognitive and emotional, which will be a giant love supply from our real self. We can finish sentences about our dreams. We can have our inner child finish sentences, also. There is no limit to the way we can use this valuable method.

On the following page is a chart called the U-turn showing one way we can use finishing sentences as a love supply from our real self.

Praying as Catharsis
6. Another way you can dump your garbage is to tell God how you feel. It's OK to cry or to be angry in prayer. God understands the feelings of pain and anger and frustration that come to us in this Earth School. We were meant to experience these things, so don't think that prayer has to be only thankfulness or great respect and adoration. God doesn't expect you to be perfect like Pollyanna. Besides, he already knows how you feel even before you pray. Praying is for you, not for him.

Dumping your own garbage is very healthy. It is a sign of real self-strength. Forget the notion that it is a sign of weakness. It is not. It will not reinforce the negative self unless you wallow in the garbage and increase it by playing the martyr role by saying "poor me" and licking your wounds in self-administered sympathy. But that isn't dumping; it is actually holding in and on to the garbage. If you savor the garbage, you will increase in sadness, hurting, and grouchiness.

By contrast, dumping will make you feel wonderfully free and uncluttered in your life. Remind yourself that everyone, every day, collects garbage. It is part of living on this earth in an environment of imperfection. The key difference between generally healthy people and emotionally "sick" people is that the healthy people don't keep garbage for very long. They refuse to believe and harbor lies about themselves, because they respect and cherish their real self. They also realize that they are experiencing a growing process in their lives.

Remember that Earth School is not an elitist club for those special few who have "made it." I know that you know this, but sometimes it doesn't hurt to remind ourselves that life is very real and sometimes demanding and hurtful. It is also very rich and rewarding when we know a few things to relieve the stress and pain.

Dumping your own garbage, by implementing a workable outlet of any of the things I've mentioned, can provide a great big love supply. In fact, this dumping process can provide the best, most effective love supply of all. Unfortunately, this is also one of the most neglected and overlooked forms of love supplies from yourself. So often we run frantically to others every time we want good love supplies, when if we would turn to our own real love source, we would find the best and most fulfilling love supplies of all. In the process, our real selves would benefit greatly.

Love Supplies From God
Of all the people we've mentioned, the ones who have also learned to rely on God for additional love supplies have the strength of steel. Sir Thomas More, the

The U-turn

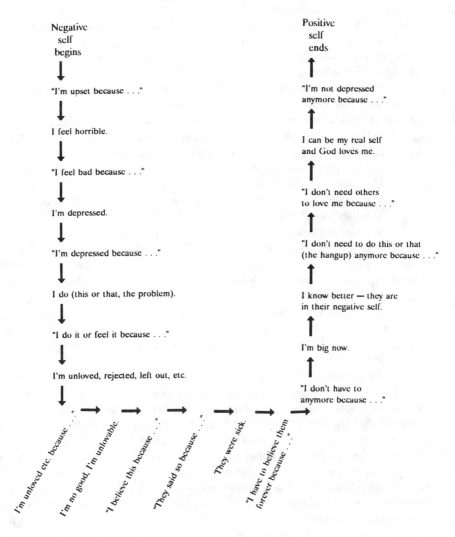

Negative
self
begins
↓
"I'm upset because . . ."
↓
I feel horrible.
↓
"I feel bad because . . ."
↓
I'm depressed.
↓
"I'm depressed because . . ."
↓
I do (this or that, the problem).
↓
"I do it or feel it because . . ."
↓
I'm unloved, rejected, left out, etc.
↓

Positive
self
ends
↑
"I'm not depressed
anymore because . . ."
↑
I can be my real self
and God loves me.
↑
"I don't need others
to love me because . . ."
↑
"I don't need to do this or that
(the hangup) anymore because . . ."
↑
I know better — they are
in their negative self.
↑
I'm big now.
↑
"I don't have to
anymore because . . ."

→ I'm unloved etc. because . . ." → I'm no good, I'm unlovable. → "I believe this because . . ." → "They said so because . . ." → They were sick. → "I have to believe them forever because . . ." →

Figure 14

famous English nobleman who was also Archbishop of Canterbury, was of these people. He was a close friend of King Henry VIII and was widely known to be a loyal, true-hearted, and deeply religious man. Because his faith in God was stronger than any other loyalty, Sir Thomas followed his own conscience on spiritual matters, not the king's orders. That cost him the king's friendship, and eventually his life.

He was in tune with his own real self and with God. He willing gave up his life rather than publicly approve the king's divorce. This went against his inner conviction, and he stood fast on the issue.

Sir Thomas More's example became widely known throughout Europe. He was a mighty man who did not need to rely on others. His strong, true, real self was fortified and made even stronger by a personal relationship with God. He allowed his real self to depend on God, and this dependence enabled him to be totally independent of other people's opinions. This is how a good dependency works. It leads to independence and self-reliance. People like Sir Thomas More need other people only so they can share and give of their real self. They love people, but remain independent and whole. They do not need anyone to fill them up, because they are for the most part already filled.

Anyone can benefit from such a healthy dependence on God. Knowing that God personally cares about each of us, and developing an ongoing relationship with Him, can make up for all the inadequate treatment we might have received while growing up. This can greatly help the real self to achieve full expression. In fact, a relationship with God is what many people in the final stages of therapy often seek. They want an ordering of the universe. A philosophy or a faith gives purpose and meaning to their new-found real self. They crave accurate religion. They seek a Higher Power to offer light and hope. This is a great indicator that they are in touch with their real self.

Prayer and meditation are primary tools to developing a companionship with God. The people who seek and find faith bring a closeness to the spiritual realm that produces joy and peace of mind. For many, this provides the greatest love supply available. For others who have been shamed and forced in their childhood in the name of religion, much deeper work must be done first before they can recognize a Higher Power. Religious fanaticism, Pollyanna religionists, fake blind conformity to religious law, pervasive rebellion against authority figures, superiority, judgmentalism, all in the name of religion, have plagued our world for centuries. These horrible substitutes for the genuine love supplies that can quietly and powerfully come from God, have deceived many wonderful people. Such confusion has hidden this *great treasure* from their view—love supplies from God.

Chapter Eight
Real Love Supplies
and Romance

Romantic love is a passionate excitement between a man and a woman. It has many parts—emotional, social, sexual, intellectual, and spiritual to mention a few. Many therapists believe only five to fifteen percent of the people are "well" enough to have this kind of love. Romantic love is where two people share from their fullness, or two full love buckets sharing from their fullness, not two empty people desperately clinging to fill up their emptiness. "Full" people are in love with their life and their turn on earth, adversity and all.

Before anyone can even think of or know what this kind of love is, they must 1) have high self-esteem or be mostly in their real selves, or have mostly rescued and reunited with the lost inner child of the past. 2) They must know what their real self is like, and this self must be *visible* to them so they know what kind of real self they are as far as interests, values, and characteristics are concerned, because not all real selves are exactly alike. And 3) they must be similar to each other, these romantic partners. Alex Smith said, "Love is but the discovery of your self in others and the delight in that recognition."

If a person finishes ten sentences: "I am a person who . . ." he will begin to be more visible to himself. If he finishes ten sentences that begin with: "One of my favorite things to do is . . .," he will see more of the kind of interests that he has. If he is mostly in his real self, these sentences will be very different than a negative self!

For a similarity, we can compare our lists of visible selves with our partner and see if there is a mate or matching self there. This helps create a spark or electricity (not chemistry) between a man and woman. It has very little to do with externals like appearances, performances, money, fame, sex, etc. It has everything to do with internals or souls or spirits. Some have called it "soul mates." It is a mystic bonding. It is very, very powerful and only a few people ever evolve enough to experience it. The others say it doesn't exist; it is a fantasy; it is only for "the romantic," it never lasts longer than twenty-four months, etc.

The false self has many substitutes for romantic love. One of the most common is parent-to-spouse tranferences. Many people marry the parent they never had, or so they suppose; later, the spouse turns out to be the same parent they did have!

Men often attract a woman who they think is very much like the mother they needed and wanted so badly and never really had. During the "romantic period" of their relationship, they have the illusion that at last unfinished business with mom is finished, and they have found a mom who truly loves them. Individually, she gives him all the permanency, exclusiveness, and possessiveness he never had and always craved. The woman feels the same, only in reverse—she has found a good dad (or parent) that she never quite had enough of. This gives her a big "spark." She thinks it is true romantic love. But after the honeymoon is over, both are soon fighting and gaming with each other, exactly as they did with that negative parent in childhood. It is very disappointing. They married to get and take. They did not have a fullness of life or of purpose and meaning to share. They gave in order to get. They expected the other to *give them* love and fill them up, and they can't. No one can but you and God.

True romance is emotional independence. Where primary dependency ends, true romantic love can begin. As Thoreau said, "When my life is complete *without you*, my friend; I will call you. You will come to a palace, not an almshouse." (An almshouse is a beggar's house.) Two full, happy, secure people are sharing that fullness with a similar visible person. Why do that? Because it is more *fun* than being alone! Aloneness is *not* miserable; it's wonderful to be with your own best friend—you—but it's even *more* wonderful to share that joy with another similar real self. This is passionate excitement. This is real spark. It is excellent, difficult, and therefore very rare. For some people, it is far better to be alone, than to have a substitute soul mate.

Now, let's refer to the chart on on page 18. Remember the Type I, II, and III relationships: I Real Self to Real Self, II Real Self to False Self, and III False Self to False Self. These are also three ways to marry and three ways to divorce. So often people come to me saying they want a divorce. They are in Type III, each mostly in their false self. Either (a) symbiotic, like a submissive pleaser, doormat, caretaker, married to a domineering partner; or (b) antisymbiotic, like two domineering, bossy people fighting, or two people in mutually threatening phobias or wounds. The more one is threatened, the more what he does to handle his threat also threatens the wound of the other. They are dependent on each other, or they wouldn't "make each other" negative. They need counseling badly —not marriage counseling, but *personal* counseling.

Marital problems are always symptoms of personal problems, and unless both partners get free of the false-self styles they survived with in childhood dysfunctional families, they can never be in Type I relationships or romantic love. Their marriage can be patched or retreaded like a tire, but eventually, under pressure, it will blow out again, or they will repeat the mess in another marriage.

Healthy people do not marry sick people. Likes attract deep down. On the surface it may seem like opposites attract, but deep down "it takes one to know one," and it takes one to marry one. I have not seen an exception to this in thirty years of full-time clinical practice.

Often we see one person advancing in therapy or reading, or seeing and hearing tapes, in a Type II relationship. This cannot last forever. Eventually two people will leave this "unequally yoked together" situation. They will leave emotionally or physically or both.

True love is the extension of yourself for your own and then for another's highest development and happiness. It is wanting and working for your own and your lover's greatest self-realization—the full being-feeling-doing person. It is *never* exploitation as in the common-mutual need marriages of our times, which end in divorce over sixty per cent of the time.

What happens when a romantic relationship is not "equals"—when one partner still needs a lot of primary love and doesn't have a full love bucket to give from? Sometimes this kind of relationship doesn't last very long because the healthier partner gets tired of always giving and being needed—being parent to the other instead of a real mate. The final outcome usually depends on what the less mature person does with the love he or she gets. If such a man or woman uses the healthy partner's real love to build his or her own real self, and perhaps gets some counseling or other help along with it, the marriage may have a good chance of lasting.

Sometimes a romantic relationship can be "equals" in the sense that neither partner has a well-developed real self. Both are deficient in love supplies. If two such people establish a strong symbiosis (where each feeds off something in the other), they can often stay together for a long time until one of them tries to break out of the symbiotic pattern. This sudden change in a once-stable symbiotic relationship often occurs when one partner starts making personal changes, such as happens in psychotherapy. If one partner is ready to change and the other is not, the changing one soon outgrows the symbiotic relationship. However, this does not necessarily mean they will need to divorce. One example of a common symbiosis is a domineering, bossy man married to an insecure, fearful woman. Each needs the other—he needs someone to control; she needs someone to tell her what to do. Another example would be a too-helpful, meddling woman and a quiet, insecure man. In these types of relationships, the negative cover-ups and substitute-self styles of the partners interlock. Their real selves don't interact very often because they're all covered up. Instead, their cover-ups interact and dominate the relationship.

Now suppose the insecure, submissive woman (Alice, we'll call her) who is married to the domineering, bossy man decides she is tired of being walked on all the time. She decides it is time for a change. She wants to get rid of her insecurity cover-up and find her real self, so she goes for therapy. But she can't get her husband to go along with the idea. "I don't have any serious problems," he says. "You go if you want to." He doesn't care about changing. He's perfectly happy with the status quo because he is top dog! Let's talk more deeply about right and wrong reasons for Alice and her husband to like and dislike each other.

There are right reasons to like someone and wrong reasons to like someone. There are right reasons to dislike someone and wrong reasons to dislike a person.

The right reason to like someone is a Type I relationship (see page 18) where you are mostly in your real self and they are as well. I have drawn this in a picture. It looks like this:

Right Reasons to Like

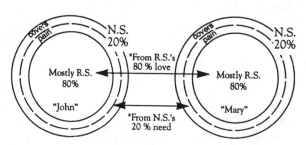

Major love target is the two real selves
(Notice how large the two RS's are.)

Figure 15

The right reason to dislike is that one person is mostly in his real self and the other is mostly in his false self. It looks like this:

Right Reason to Dislike

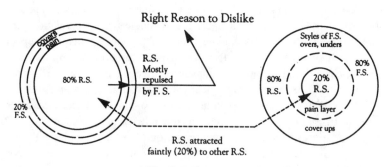

No major love target
What happens if the 20% R.S. grows?

Figure 16

It is not wrong for a real self to dislike the false self of another. It is right and good. After all, we should dislike our own negative self and all others. All other real selves should dislike our negatives, too. We are all allies in this war against false selves, ours and others'.

The wrong reason to like someone is Type III (a) (see page 18). This is symbiotic or false spark. A domineering "male chauvinist pig" (MCP) will be attracted to a submissive pleaser caretaker person who has survived poor love supplies by feeling others' feelings and not her own, sometimes called Dumb Dora Doormat or DDD. Some people write this false love in this way: MCP/DDD.

I have drawn this frequently for my patients who are in a "sick" relationship. It looks like this:

Wrong Reasons to Like

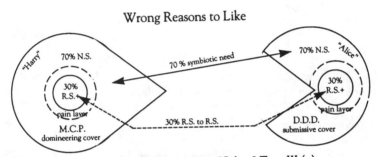

Major love target is two negative "Selves" Type III (a)
(Outside, opposites attract; inside, likes attract)
Notice what happens to N.S.'s as 2 R.S's grow (R.S. and N.S. shrinks).

Figure 17

The wrong reason to dislike is two negative selves who are antisymbiotic or Type III (b) (see page 18). This means the two false-self styles of these people do not attract, they repel. They do not go together like Type III (a). People often experience this as dislike, even hate, or contempt. It can happen as a personality clash or dissonance between two people, often called incompatible. It can happen between *any* two people: children and parents, siblings, rebels and rebels, pleasers and pleasers, husbands and wives, boss and manager, student and teacher. The list goes on.

There are two solutions: one external, the other internal. One is a patch—superficial, temporary. The other, deeper, more difficult and rare. It is to get into your real self, both of you ideally, but even if it's just you, it's better than no one. It is better to dislike someone for the right reasons than for the wrong. I have often drawn this for classes and patients. It looks like this:

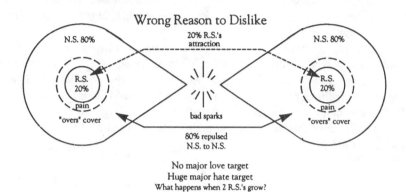

Figure 18

Know the truth and the truth will make you free. Know which of these four you are in. There are good and bad reasons for quitting anything. Think of someone you like or dislike and go deep under the surface of the water, like the iceberg, and fix the deep feelings and causes. Remember, "I forgive scorpions, but I don't put them down my neck."

Look carefully at the diagrams of *wrong reasons* to like or dislike (Type III), and imagine that just one of them (you) went to counseling or therapy and the real self —twenty to thirty percent—began to grow to fifty or sixty percent. Now the diagrams begin looking more and more like the ones in *right reasons* to like or dislike.

Then you will see the solutions to so many external problems and hangups, myriads of them, beginning to change. Problems we have been working on all our lives begin to give way. Problems with spouse, children, employers, friends, colleagues, and so on. All of these begin to take on a brand new perspective and size. Yes, knowledge is power and ignorance is helplessness. It begins with cognitive or head knowledge and ends up with deep experiential feeling. It takes both to make the change.

So this woman (Alice, we've called her) works hard, and after several months of therapy she begins to feel quite good about herself. However, there are more fights at home now because she doesn't give up control of herself anymore. Her symbiosis with her husband is disrupted! He doesn't understand why she's not so "dependable" now; she's different—and he doesn't like the change.

At this point Alice wonders, "What should I do? I'm in an unhealthy marriage with someone who doesn't know how to share good love supplies, which I would like." Lots of people in therapy ask this question, or one very similar to it:

How do I handle my "sick" parents, my "sick" friends, or my "sick" spouse? The answer is to take the initiative to improve the relationship yourself! Work on developing your real self first; then you can help others develop their real selves. You can give to them after you get yourself filled up. Pretty soon you'll both be giving each other real love supplies instead of cheap substitutes. You'll break out of the symbiotic patterns. Of course, if your friend or spouse doesn't want to change, you can't do much to help. In that case, you can continue giving good love supplies, but you can't waste your life "casting pearls before swine." Sooner or later, you will leave them to their fate.

Divorce

People often ask me if I believe in divorce. They want to know whether I ever tell people that they should get divorced. Sometimes I do, but usually I don't. Why? For most people, divorce is just an escape from something they think they can't handle. If they "can't handle it," that shows they think they are helpless, that their real self is not in charge. They don't have a thick skin—the personal independence and self-reliance that would make them invulnerable to most of the criticism of others. A healthy person *cannot* be emotionally hurt by another, because their emotions are controlled from inside, not outside.

Think about who really causes your feelings: she does not humiliate you; you humiliate yourself (or allow yourself to be humiliated because you believe a lie about yourself). You allow her negative self to get your negative self started. You let her lies pierce your pain layer and make big wounds. If you can learn to recognize how wonderful and valuable you really are, you'll develop a thicker skin. Then you won't need her approval so much, and she won't have power to hurt you anymore. Most criticism is garbage—dumping, anyway.

After people in therapy get their love buckets mostly filled up because they learn how beautiful and precious they really are, then I say, "Okay, now do you still want a divorce?" Usually the answer is something like this: "Why should I get a divorce? I'm happier; I give more love to my children now, and the whole atmosphere is better. My husband (or wife) isn't that bad—he recognizes that he can't hurt my feelings anymore, so he doesn't really try to." And they stay together. This is peaceful coexistence. It is not Type I. It is not romantic love. But it is good enough for many people.

Some people would say that it is better to leave the marriage at this point and be with someone else to share *all* of your fullness. They say that such a change would even be better for the children. Sometimes that is true. Sometimes the pain and ugliness of separation and the loneliness and sense of failure that results from most sick divorces are high prices to pay for the hope of a new and better love relationship. Remember, you take your problems with you. Whatever parts of your negative self hurt the first relationship will be right there with you, alive and kicking, in your new relationship, making the same kinds of problems. I say, don't divorce until you don't "need" to divorce. Once you know you are not running away or escaping, that's the time to decide about a divorce.

Now there are major exceptions to all of this. If the hurting you are experiencing is also more than emotional—if your spouse is pointing a gun at you, beating or choking you, or molesting you or your children—then you should leave right away. Don't wait to develop a thick skin if you are in physical danger. Get a divorce now. And that also applies to damage so severe that you can't grow in therapy without a separation first. I do believe in warranted divorce, just like I believe in rectifying horrible mistakes.

Despite all the publicity given to unhappy marriages and the great number of them, a healthy marriage can be by far the most full, satisfying, and loving relationship any of you will ever experience. The potential for greater and greater fullness, for permanent, mutual love, and for infinite sharing and giving exists within every healthy marriage relationship. Healthy marriage increases freedom; sick marriage decreases freedom.

Spencer W. Kimball has said:

"In a marriage commenced and based upon reasonable standards, there are no combinations of power which can destroy it *except* the power within either or both of the spouses themselves . . . . Other people and agencies may influence for good or bad. Financial, social, political, and other situations may seem to have a bearing; but the marriage depends first and always on the two spouses who can always make their marriage successful and happy, if they are determined, unselfish, and righteous.

"For every friction, there is a cause; and whenever there is unhappiness, each should search *self* to find the cause or at least that portion of the cause which originated in that self. (See why I don't believe in "marriage counseling" but rather "personal counseling?")

". . . The mortal body would soon be emaciated and die if there were not frequent feedings. The tender flower would wither and die without food and water. And so love, also, cannot be expected to last forever unless it is continually fed with portions of love . . . . Certainly the foods most vital for love are consideration, kindness, thoughtfulness, concern, expressions of affection, embraces of appreciation, admiration, pride, companionship, confidence, faith, partnership, and equality.

"If one is forever seeking the interest, comforts, and happiness of the other, the love found in courtship and cemented in marriage will grow into mighty proportions . . . Ask yourself, 'What am I giving to the relationship?'"

Much of Spencer Kimball's advice is good. If we ask ourselves, "What am I giving to the relationship?" we will be focusing on our real selves. How strong is my real self? How able to serve? How full? And if we find that we are, indeed, giving with no thought for what we will receive, we will also find ourselves rewarded in full and our love multiplied. Givers always end up with the most. We will want more of it, not less. We will be magnified by a love that grows more wholesome, more true, and more deep, a love untainted by need or want, free from conditions and restraints. Such a love is the greatest gift that one human being can give himself or another.

Part Three
CONCLUSION

Chapter Nine
The Real You

There was once an old farmer who raised chickens on his farm and who had, among his hundreds of hens, an eagle. This full-grown bird had fallen out of its nest when very young and the farmer had happened along, picked it up, and brought it home to be raised in his chicken coop. The eagle had always acted just like a chicken, and the farmer was satisfied that it always would.

One day a naturalist from a nearby zoological institute came out to see this curious phenomenon. He was surprised to see an eagle living among chickens. The farmer told him, "Though it has the body of an eagle, it's really a chicken. I've trained it to be a chicken. It's no longer an eagle."

But the naturalist protested, "It's an eagle. It has the heart of an eagle. Let me take it up on this fence, and I will show you how it will fly." So he lifted the eagle up on the fence and said to it, "Eagle, thou art an eagle. Stretch forth thy wings and fly."

The eagle looked at the man, and then back at the chicken coop where he had been raised, then jumped down off the fence to be with the chickens. The farmer said, "I told you it was a chicken."

The naturalist persuaded the farmer to let him come back the next day and try again, even though the farmer still insisted, "It's a chicken." So the next day the man lifted the eagle again, taking him to the top of the house, and spoke to him: "Eagle, thou art an eagle. Thou dost belong to the sky and not to earth. Stretch forth thy wings and fly." Again the big bird looked around at the man and down at the chicken coop which had always been his home. Then he jumped down onto the roof of the chicken coop.

The naturalist was determined to try once more. He said to the farmer, "Give me one more chance, and I'll prove to you that this is an eagle. I'll come back tomorrow and that eagle will soar," to which the farmer replied, "It's a chicken."

But the third day the naturalist came again, only this time he took the eagle away to the foot of a high mountain where he could no longer see the chicken coop. There he held this great bird, pointing his head directly into the sun, and spoke: "Eagle, thou art an eagle! Thou dost belong to the sky and not to the earth. Stretch forth thy wings and fly." This time, the eagle stared into the sun, its great body trembling, moved its massive wings, slowly at first, and then with the mighty screech of an eagle, it flew.

This fable is much like the story of the lion who thought he was a lamb, except that the outcome is totally different. The eagle found someone who helped him to realize what and who he *really* was. The naturalist knew that the eagle's buried real self understood its true identity and would respond to the truth if it were given enough of the right opportunities to grow. And it did. Instead of continuing to live a lie as a chicken, or merely pretending to be big and strong, as the lamb-lion did, the eagle eventually listened to its real self, believed in it, and flew—the most natural thing for an eagle to do (and something a chicken would never do).

Uncovering Is Becoming

Just like the eagle, your real self already knows the truth—that you are immeasurably beautiful, powerful, compassionate, and tender—and can respond to the command to fly, to actualize in full-grown stature what is already in embryo. It just takes good, real love supplies from others and from oneself, some time, patience, and persistence (lots of it). Uncovering one's beautiful real self beneath the garbage layer or the cloud layer is like gradually uncovering a large, exquisite and priceless oil painting which has been wrapped in a layer of very heavy paper or cardboard.

If you manage to cut a small hole in the paper about three inches in diameter, you may not be very excited by what little of the painting you can see through the hole, even though the person who helped you cut the hole says, "Look at that! Aren't those colors beautiful?" If you work and enlarge the hole so it is even twice as big, you probably still won't be able to appreciate very much of the beauty of the painting. You may not even be motivated to keep cutting then because it takes so much effort.

But if you persevere and finally get nearly half of the paper off, then you begin to see part of the painting's beauty and to develop some feelings of excitement and desire about the parts you still can't see. This is hope faith. You begin to believe that this may indeed be the most beautiful painting you will ever see, and from then on you want to work day and night to uncover the rest because you believe it will be worth every bit of your effort—and it will.

In just this way, once you glimpse the truth and the beauty of your real identity, you will want to see all of it *more than you want anything else.* And then the struggle to uncover your real self won't be as hard as it was in the beginning.

If you find and associate with people who can give you good love supplies—like empathy and openness and firmness—and stay away from those who only give cheap substitutes, if you study your negative styles in order to gain more control over them, if you monitor your thoughts and disown the ones that come from your negative self, and if you give yourself good love supplies by meditating, visualizing, and dumping your garbage, then you will discover your strong and beautiful real self under the pain layer. And it will be as a priceless and exquisite painting, made even more valuable by the effort and hard work of uncovering it.

As with most valuable things, you'll love it because you worked hard for it and sacrificed much for it. And you will reunite with your inner child and love him or her forever. As Jesus said, "Except ye become as a little child, you cannot enter into the kingdom of Heaven."

You Are Not What You Do

Remember that you are not your performances, not you appearance and not your adversity. You are a beautiful, feeling spirit being, brought here from another dimension for a specific learning experience. Most of us get mixed up or forget entirely who we are because we are taught to equate ourselves with our performances—and then we think our failure at some project or role or performance means failure in life.

Try this experiment to see if you can separate yourself from your actions. (It won't help you at all if you just read the steps of the experiment. You have to do each step as you read. So get a piece of paper and a pencil right now.) Draw a circle about the size of an orange in the middle of a piece of paper. Write "me" in the middle of the circle and then draw eight spokes radiating out from the circle like the spokes of a wheel. At the end of each spoke, draw a smaller circle, about the size of a fifty-cent piece.

Now, think of some of the hundreds of roles you slip into and out of each day: cook, student, mother or father, mechanic, teacher, friend, husband or wife, lover, lawyer, counselor, dishwasher, gardener. Put whatever roles most often apply to you in the small outer circles, one to each circle, so that you have eight of the roles listed. Next, try to rate your performance in each of these roles, on a scale of one to ten. How is your performance as a cook lately? It it's tops, put a ten in the circle; it it's terrible, put a one. Do this with every role, putting a rating in every circle.

Now pause a minute and look at the center circle. Can you put a number in the center circle? Try it. Rate "me" on a scale of one to ten. What did you write? There's only one right answer this time, and that is the number ten. Your unique, independent spirit identity is separate from and unaffected by any performance in any of your roles; it is that of a lovable, capable, beautiful inner being—and it has to be rated a "ten." That's the only rating consistent with the truth about you. If you don't have a ten in the inner circle, you will never be able to be a ten in any of the outer circles.

Less-than-perfect performances in our roles in life are to be expected. They are normal. They can't affect personal worth in any way at all. We have to constantly keep reminding ourselves of that because of our society's belief that failures and mistakes make us bad. In reality, failures and mistakes are specifically given to us in this trial-and-error Earth School to *help us learn*. One great man said, "No defeat is final—it's only preparation for the next and greater victory."

Believing in the Real You

Remember how we said your problems can be your servants? That's why problems exist—to teach and encourage you to grow. When used in the right way—working and striving to master them—you gain strength and power. Your real-self capability is enhanced; it grows greater. When you use it in the wrong way, you become bitter and cynical, or you feel beaten and decide not to stick your neck out any more. What a sad thing for a beautiful and infinitely capable being to give up!

In reality, your potential for good, for power and wisdom and sensitivity and influence, is beyond your furthest imaginings. If you could see your real self, given the right kind of treatment, even just ten years from now, you would be in awe. You would give up all your negative self styles, no matter how comfortable they have become, to have that real self. You would want it more than you wanted anything else. And you would be willing to endure all the sweat and pain and tears it takes to get rid of the negative layers covering your beautiful self. Why? Because that awesome person of the future, that fully uncovered oil painting, is the *real you*.

Is the struggle worth the price? Yes. Your worth is beyond price. And beyond time, or space. Spread your wings and fly!

Chapter Ten
Sterling Quotes

Here are quotes on the following pages that are either original quotes by Dr. Sterling Ellsworth or from other sources of inspiration. Ponder them and give heed to the wisdom that is deeply expressed in many of these interesting insights into human nature. Much can be gained by applying simple but profound principles and sayings.

Performances do not equal
your worth.

Earth birth equals worth.

If you need to marry to fill
your emptiness,
you will marry trouble.

Sex is a minor part of a healthy,
romantic relationship.

Soul mates come in real-self
(not perfect) packages.

Healthy people *play* at life;
sick people *work* at life.

Real love begins
where dependency ends.

Strait is the gate and narrow the
way, and few there be that enter.
(*Jesus*)

There is nothing quite so powerful
as real gentleness,
and nothing quite so gentle as genuine power. (*McKay*)

The things you crave will come to
you when you don't crave them
anymore.

He who will save his life shall lose
it, and he who would lose his life
(lets go) will save it. (*Jesus*)

No pain no gain,
or some pain some gain.

The masses are asses
(in their false self).

SOS . . . Shrink or Split

No one has anything I want;
everything I need
is in my own heart.

True love conquers all things. False
love ruins all things.

Know the truth
and the truth will make you free,
but it may make you miserable first.

All mistakes are learning devices.
You have the right to fail
and to succeed.

True marriage increases
your personal freedom;
sick marriage decreases freedom.

When we are in our false self
it is a childhood repeat.

I built a whole city
where I didn't even need
a fence post.

Don't squirt perfume over garbage.

You can't fight an enemy
you can't see.

A person in a hurry
is usually in a negative.

I'd rather be in neutral
than reverse.

You won't get an "A" in the Earth
School of Hard Knocks by going to
your grave repeating childhood
survival styles of your false self.

On the outside opposites attract;
on the inside likes attract.

The Human Feeling Identity Seed
can only be nourished by real love.

No amount of suffering is wasted;
all of it will strengthen
weaknesses we have.

Do not burn a cathedral
to fry an egg.

Caretakers care in order to take.

When in doubt as to what to say, do
empathy.

True romance is two mostly full
people (full love buckets)
sharing from their fullness,
never two empty people desperately
taking to fill their emptiness.

Good dependencies lead to good
independence; bad dependencies
lead to fake independence or
chronic dependence.

It's an honor to be the enemy
of all negative selves.

No (mom, dad, friend, man,
woman) is better than a bad one.

Many things (food, sex, money,
success, failure) can be a wonderful
servant or a horrible master.

All stress is self made, because our
own frustrated expectations
precede all weirdness.

Feelings are the engine to life's
train, and performances are the
caboose. Don't pull your train
backwards by the caboose.

To deny is to lie.

Love has no purpose but itself.
When you love in order to get, the
love light goes out
and the *need* light goes on.

True love is purposeless
and useless.

Crying works wonders!

What others think of me is none of
my business.

Real forgiveness must be preceded
by in depth re-experiencing
of childhood fears, anger, and pain
which turn into pity,
then forgiveness of our abusers.

I forgive scorpions, but I don't put
them down my neck.
(*Joseph F. Smith*)

Superficial forgiveness is a feeling
stopper.

"I don't know" really means
"Let me see."

The good or bad you do comes back
to you.

Neither a scrooge nor a patsy be.

Over-reacting and underacting are
the false self.

No one can upset us unless
they have something we want.

People who keep you in your head
or away from feelings are terrified
of their own deep feelings.

Birds of a feather flock together.

It takes one to know one.

Full togetherness comes from
full aloneness and vice versa.

You don't love an oasis in the
desert . . . you need it.

Negative selves compare and
compete for love substitutes.

Feed a man a fish and you feed him
for a day; teach him to fish and you
feed him for a lifetime.

Some forms of "therapy" are great
cognitive mazes that keep people
away from their feelings;
true psychotherapy is re-experiencing childhood and adult pain,
anger, and fear with a safe,
supportive person.

"Feeling stoppers" keep the
negative self in power
and prostitute our feeling
identity seed.

Things excellent are difficult as they
are rare. (*Spinoza*)

Don't seek storms; they will
come to you all by themselves.

Winning over our negative self
is our greatest learning device.

The self-actualizing person, in the
midst of intense emotion, weeps.

Don't die dumb!

Give your real self equal time on
the TV of your mind;
never let the false self have
the last word.

Impatience comes from doubt and
patience comes from certainty.

Procrastination comes from fear
of failure and/or rebellion.

Too much external orderliness com-
pensates for and
covers up too much internal
(feeling) disorderliness.

My wonder child was in
a feeling prison.

Time and bodies
are learning devices.

If the past can rule the present, as if
there were no time, then the present
can go back and heal the past, as if
there were no time.

*You cannot fix internals
with externals.*

Your life is a school from birth to
death. If you're alive, you still need
to be here in Earth School.

Different strokes for different folks.

The part of us that looks
for the real self
is the one we are looking for.

It takes more strength to honestly
feel your feelings
than to hide them.

Strive and strain
and ruin your brain.

Males and females internally
are very much alike.

God makes no junk people:
they do it themselves.

Beauty is in the eye
of the beholder (and so is ugly).

Crying is strength;
hiding and denying are weak.

Negative thought and feeling
detection leads to positive thought
and feeling selection.

Blame is shame;
mistakes are learning devices;
learning is often unlearning.

Thank you for the feedback. I'll
take it under advisement with
my beautiful self.

I might have made a mistake, but
I'm still a good person.

True love is the discovery of
yourself in others, and the delight in
that recognition. (*Alex Smith*)

The way out is in or through.

Most problems are not caused
or solved by what we *do* but by
what we *feel*.

Li'l kids run completely on
love supplies;
they are li'l radar love machines.

Are you a human being
or a human doing?

As we do therapy,
we lose old "friends."

I can tell where I am by the kind
of people that turn on to me.

Great spirits have always
encountered violent opposition from
mediocre minds. (*Einstein*)

Children need no discipline but
the discipline of love. (*Montague*)

See the mark upon the path (your
vision), and you're halfway there.

True humanness is an intimate blend
of tenderness and power.

Float like a butterfly,
sting like a bee.
(*Mohammed Ali*)

Nothing can drain you unless
it has something you *need*.

Rebels always have a place where
they please, and pleasers a place
where they rebel.

Rebels and pleasers
are false selves.

True therapy is love given
and love received.

"Rescuers" usually give
in order to get.

Often the thing we hate we cause.

Sex without love
estranges two people. (*Fromm*)

Love has no fruits but love itself.

Hope springs eternal
in the human breast.

Don't divorce to escape your own
vulnerability to your partner;
get invulnerable first, then decide.

Weak people lie about feelings
and hide;
strong people face them honestly.

Feel your own feelings
and not always someone else's.

This above all,
to your own self be true.

Emotional independence often
comes from adult real self loving
and rescuing the wounded child
within.

The angry person
is a suffering person (*Fromm*)

To *need* is to take;
to want is to share.

I "need" (want) you because
I love you, or I love you
because I *need* you?

Need mates are not soul mates.

If success equals our worth,
failure equals no worth.

All bullies have been bullied.

Live and learn, crash and burn,
get up and take another turn.

Healthy people ask
that their needs be met.

Spouses and children are giving
places; self, God, and other friends
are taking places!

Finishing sentences is a love supply
from your real self,
if you go far enough.

Identifying with our abusers gives
us fake power to escape from
childhood helplessness.

Whenever you are mostly in your
false self, go back to
your inner child and look for
repeats, and let your real self
give the child love . . . now.

The self your body obeys the most
becomes the largest.

You're one in a million
(and I'm the other one).

Strive and strain takers
are always tired; givers are calmer
and have lots of energy.

Givers always end up
with the most.

Perfection is heading
in the right direction.

Know, feel, and understand all your
feelings, but obey only
real-self feelings.

Look for the fun
in each thing you do. (*Kimball*)

We often think we have married the
parent we didn't have, and after the
honeymoon they later become the
one we did have.

I ain't well, but I sure am better.
(*Lair*)

The parent the client first brings up
(in therapy) is often
not the worst one.

You're in charge of your mouth;
I'm in charge of my ears.

If you have blue glasses on,
everything you see turns blue.

Caretaker versus caregivers.

By the inch it's a cinch;
by the yard it's too hard.

Don't confuse me
with my body suit.

Man is that he might have joy.

Never try to teach your pig to sing.
It will only frustrate you
and annoy the pig.

It is only with the heart that one can
see rightly; what is essential
is invisible to the eye. (*St. Exupery*)

You can never get enough
of what you don't need.

Your adversity is *not* your identity.

Most problems are not caused
or solved by what we *do* but by
what we *feel*.

Are you a human being
or a human doing?

As we do therapy,
we lose old "friends."

I can tell where I am by the kind
of people that turn on to me.

It takes more strength to honestly
feel your feelings
than to hide them.

Great spirits have always
encountered violent opposition from
mediocre minds. (*Einstein*)

Children need no discipline but
the discipline of love. (*Montague*)

See the mark upon the path (your
vision), and you're halfway there.

True humanness is an intimate blend
of tenderness and power.

Float like a butterfly,
sting like a bee.
(*Mohammed Ali*)

Nothing can drain you unless
it has something you *need*.

Rebels always have a place where
they please, and pleasers a place
where they rebel.

Rebels and pleasers
are false selves.

True therapy is love given
and love received.

"Rescuers" usually give
in order to get.

Often the thing we hate we cause.

Sex without love
estranges two people. (*Fromm*)

Love has no fruits but love itself.

Li'l kids run completely on
love supplies;
they are li'l radar love machines.

Hope springs eternal
in the human breast.

Don't divorce to escape your own
vulnerability to your partner;
get invulnerable first, then decide.

Weak people lie about feelings
and hide;
strong people face them honestly.

Feel your own feelings
and not always someone else's.

This above all,
to your own self be true.

Emotional independence often
comes from adult real self loving
and rescuing the wounded child
within.

The angry person
is a suffering person (*Fromm*)

To *need* is to take;

We can't take care of others if we
can't take care of ourselves.

A gift to be a gift must be
accepted; otherwise, it is a burden
to the other person.

Most people are unaware
of the path they are on.

Tears from real feelings
release us from our armor.

Becoming is letting go of what
you are not (your false self).

Flexible expectations
decrease anger and pain.

When we learn to *accept* instead of
expect, we have fewer
disappointments.

If we truly accept what and who we
are, it doesn't matter what other
people say.

Most of us are trapped
in our own armor.

Being quiet
is more than not talking.

Being well is more
than the absence of a cold.

Healthy people have a few deep
friends. Sick people have a lot of
superficial friends or none.
(*Maslow*)

Sick people are afraid to be alone or
to have "nothing to do."

They live in the past and the
future, never the precious present.

Since I know myself, I can know
you. We are all part of each other in
our real selves.

I cannot know the unknown if to the
known I cling. (*Fisher*)

The true self is much more real than
the one we have been calling "I" all
these years.

Have we mistaken need for love?
Need takes to fill our emptiness,
and love shares from our fullness.

How would you be *better* than
others when they were all born as
beautiful, innocent, and perfect
as you were. (*Fisher*)

It is necessary to separate need from
greed.

Ambition from the heart (real self)
is pure. It competes with no one and
harms no one. (win-win)

Stand still more often
and appreciate, rather than
run around and grab.

She was born good, kind, and
loving; therefore,
she didn't have to fear or doubt.

If we honestly face our false self,
there is a little chance it may
destroy us temporarily; but if we do
not face it, it will *certainly*
destroy us eventually.

We must say, "Come back
whenever you want, false self,
But each time you do,
"I (real me) will be stronger
and you will be weaker."

True forgiveness is always
preceded by strong desire,
complete purging of pain and
anger, then *pity* and sorrow for the
"scorpion" which we forgive,
but never put down our neck.

Good people, especially children,
love to be with us when we love
and live in the present, not the past
or the future. This is the greatest
present of all.

We must know our past
and prepare for our future,
but *live* in our present.

Time, as we know it here on earth,
is a learning device.

Pain is the difference between what
is and what I want it to be. (Spencer
Johnson)

Our pain and anger come from
frustrated expectations.

Love is to a child like sunshine is to
a flower (snarl and they wilt).

He who cannot see God in the face
of a little child is blind.

I want a person who "sees" my
body the same way he thinks about
his own body—not as a sex object.

He who lives by the flesh
will die by the flesh.

The spirit self is the primary love
target in all healthy relationships;
the body is a minor part only.

If the masses are asses,
who wants to be *popular*?

Choosing friends and mates by
externals only is "going after
the lust of your eyes."

True sexual expression must be
preceded by emotional, verbal,
and non-sexual physical union,
which are constant and permanent.

Trials and tribulations are mandato-
ry, but misery is optional.

No one's body is a ticket to glory.

If you can possibly say "Yes" to a
child, do it. (*Emma McKay*)

God binds us temporarily to free us
permanently, Satan "frees" us
temporarily to bind us
permanently.

You cannot heal
what you cannot *feel*.